John Bachelder

Popular resorts and how to reach them

Combining a brief description of the principal summer retreats in the United States

John Bachelder

Popular resorts and how to reach them
Combining a brief description of the principal summer retreats in the United States

ISBN/EAN: 9783337147624

Printed in Europe, USA, Canada, Australia, Japan

Cover: Foto ©Andreas Hilbeck / pixelio.de

More available books at **www.hansebooks.com**

POPULAR RESORTS,

AND HOW TO REACH THEM.

COMBINING A BRIEF DESCRIPTION OF THE

PRINCIPAL SUMMER RETREATS IN THE UNITED STATES,

AND THE

ROUTES OF TRAVEL LEADING TO THEM.

BY

JOHN B. BACHELDER,

AUTHOR OF "THE ILLUSTRATED TOURISTS' GUIDE," "GETTYSBURG, WHAT TO SEE, AND HOW TO SEE IT," "THE ISOMETRICAL DRAWING OF THE GETTYSBURG BATTLEFIELD," "DESCRIPTIVE KEY TO THE PAINTING OF LONGSTREET'S ASSAULT AT GETTYSBURG," DESIGNER OF THE HISTORICAL PAINTINGS OF THE BATTLE OF GETTYSBURG, LAST HOURS OF LINCOLN, &C.

Illustrated by One Hundred Wood-Cuts

BY THE BEST ENGRAVERS,

MANY OF THEM FROM ORIGINAL SKETCHES BY JOHN B. BACHELDER.

BOSTON:
JOHN B. BACHELDER, PUBLISHER.
41-45 FRANKLIN STREET
(At Lee & Shepard's.)

1874.

Entered, according to Act of Congress, in the year 1874, by
JOHN B. BACHELDER,
In the Office of the Librarian of Congress, at Washington

ELECTROTYPED AND PRINTED BY RAND, AVERY, & CO.,
117 FRANKLIN STREET, BOSTON.

PREFACE.

To know *how* to travel is a matter of great importance to the tourist. Many persons pass unheeded by the picturesque beauties of a pleasant route, expecting to find the combined pleasures, which others have described, awaiting them at the end of their journey. In some instances where the points visited are places of celebrity, and the route of approach lies through an uninteresting region, like many of our ocean watering-places, this is the case. In others, as much pleasure may be derived *en route* as can be expected on our arrival. This is particularly true of mountain travel, where every turn opens up new and interesting scenes.

Where a single excursion is to be made for the season, it is a matter of importance for the tourist to select a route of travel, the peculiarities of which are congenial to his tastes. Public resorts, which may furnish abundant sources of pleasure to one person, frequently present little of interest to another. While one would be satisfied with a single day at the sea-shore, another would never tire of watching the waves break upon a rock-bound coast. The rugged grandeur of the mountain rocks, and deepening mystery of the glens, which to many prove sources of great delight, for others have no attractions. Hence the importance of choosing desirable " Popular Resorts, and Routes to Reach Them."

Of all the celebrated watering-places on the coast, or frequented mountain-houses, no two are alike, yet each locality possesses an individual interest; and the routes which lead to them have their attractions, either in the safety and comforts afforded the traveller, or in the picturesque beauty of the region through which they pass. It is to lay this plainly before the public that these pages are presented.

PREFACE TO SECOND EDITION.

THE satisfactory reception of the first edition of this work, and the universal request of patrons for its continuance, have determined the author to publish, *annually*, a volume devoted exclusively to the interests of travel, which shall give, not only general information regarding "Popular Resorts, and How to Reach Them," thus obviating the necessity of wading through a large number of local Guide Books, but furnish a standard medium through which proprietors or agents, who represent houses or routes, may describe or illustrate the merits of their respective interests. The illustrated descriptions of this volume have been prepared from personal observation, while the "item" notices have either been written expressly for it, or compiled from the best published accounts. Brief descriptions of other resorts throughout the country, with means for reaching them, are solicited for the next edition, the compilation of which will be commenced immediately on the publication of this. Illustrated descriptions, with superior wood-cuts, furnished on application.

The country abounds in charming retreats, at present unknown to the tourist, which may thus be developed and made popular.

This work does not give time-tables: for these the tourist is recommended to supply himself with THE TRAVELER'S OFFICIAL GUIDE, before commencing his journey.

J. B. B.

CONTENTS.

Camping Out	9–11
Harbor and Coastwise Excursions	11
North Conway	12–16
Boston and Maine Railroad	17–31
Cooperstown, N.Y.; Trenton Falls, N.Y.; Straw's Point, N.H.; Rocky Point, R.I.	32
Long Branch, N.J.; Greenwood Lake, N.Y.	33
Pennsylvania Scenery — Central Railroad of New Jersey	34–53
Doubling Gap, White Sulphur Springs, Penn.; York Springs, Penn.; Mount Holly Springs, Penn.; Alexandria Bay, N.Y.; Thousand Islands; Salem, Mass.	54
Cape May — West Jersey Railroad	55–57
Atlantic City, N.J. — Camden and Atlantic Railroad	58–63
Bedford Springs, Penn.; Bellows Falls, Vt.; Prout's Neck, Me.; Old Orchard Beach, Me.	64
Portland, Me.; Cushing's Island, Me.; Genesee Falls, N.Y.; Sharon Springs, N.Y.; Taghkanic Falls, N.Y.; Portsmouth, N.H.; Frost's Point, N.H.	65
Western Travel — Chicago, Burlington, and Quincy Railroad	66–68
Mount Desert, Me.	68
Lynn, Mass.; Swampscott, Mass.; Deer Island, Me.; Seneca Falls, N.Y.; Suspension Bridge, N.Y.; Casco Bay, Me.	69
Sharon Springs, N.Y.; Tekaharawa Falls, N.Y.; Howe's Cave, Little Bear's Head, N.H.; Stonington, R.I.; Newburyport, Mass.; Plum Island, Mass.	70
Northern Central Railway	71–88
Isles of Shoals, N.H.; Narraganset Pier, R.I.; Marblehead, Mass.; Lowell Island, Mass.; Tinker's Island, New London, Conn.	89
Ebensburg, Penn.; Chelsea, Mass.; Chelsea (Revere) Beach, Mass.; Hampton, N.H.	90
Boston, Concord, and Montreal Railroad	91–122
Richfield Springs, N.Y.; Glen's Falls, N.Y.; Nahant, Mass.	123
Lake George, N.Y.; The "Glen," N.H.; York Beach, Me.; Watch Hill Point, R.I.	124

CONTENTS.

Pennsylvania Railroad 125–137

  New York City and Vicinity. Up the Hudson 138–139
  Vicinity of New York: Long Island, N.Y.; New Lebanon Springs, N.Y.; Columbia Springs, N.Y.; Lake George, N.Y. . 140

Excursion through Long Island Sound — Stonington Line . . 141–142

  City of Boston 143
  Scarborough Beach, Me.; Rye Beach, N.H.; Adirondacks, N.Y.; Portage, N.Y. 144

Shelter Island, N.Y. 145–150

  Saratoga Springs, N.Y. 151–153
  Niagara Falls, Quebec, &c. 153, 154
  Clifton Springs, N.Y. 154

North Mountain House, Penn. 155–163

  VIRGINIA SPRINGS — Augusta Springs, Bath Alum Springs, Capon Springs, Healing Springs, Hot Springs, Jordan Rock Alum Springs, Montgomery White Sulphur Springs, Rawley Springs, Rockbridge Alum Springs, Rockbridge Baths, Sweet Springs, Warm Springs, Yellow Sulphur Springs, Greenbrier White Sulphur Springs 164
  Gloucester, Mass.; Rockport, Mass.; Moosehead Lake, Falls of Montmorenci, Saguenay River 165

Excursion to Oak Bluffs and Katama 166–176

  Land of the Pilgrims — Old Colony Railroad 177–186
  Lake Champlain, Plattsburg, N.Y. 186

CAMPING OUT.

BEYOND all question, the most delightful and healthful way to spend one's summer vacation is in "camping out," provided the weather is reasonably pleasant. A time of storm is gloomy enough, whatever the mode chosen for enjoyment.

CAMPING OUT.

In "camping out," all the stiff formalities of conventional life are put aside. The body is left free for any sort of dress except fashionable styles; and the mind is in constant and cheery repose, and therefore able to enjoy life with the keenest zest. Health comes to the invalid, with its building-up force of a sharp and eager appetite; and the strong feel an electric energy, daily renewed, unknown in great cities and marts of trade. In fact, while the visitor to thronged summer-resorts often returns home worn and wearied, the sojourner of the camp comes back increased in his avoirdupois, his strength, and his sense of having had a "glorious" vacation.

"Camping out" means a sort of woodman's or frontier life. It means living in a tent; sleeping on boughs or leaves; cooking your own meals; washing your own dishes, and clothes perhaps; getting up your own fuel; making your own fire; and foraging for your own provender. It means activity, variety, novelty, and fun alive; and the more you have of it, the more you like it; and the longer you stay, the less willing you are to give it up. In fact, there is no glory for the summer tourist, to compare with the "camping-out" glory.

For preparation, you will first know where your camp is to be, and what it affords for your pleasure. And you will scarcely make your party less than three, nor more than five. If the number exceeds five, it will be better to pitch two distinct camps at some distance apart, and thus have pleasant "neighbors" to visit, and hospitable parties to give, each to the other. Guns and fishing tackle carefully prepared for use will, of course, be required for localities where game and fish abound; and few places would be selected where one or the other, at least, would not be accessible. Two grand essentials should be thoughtfully remembered, — plenty of dish-cloths, and a good hatchet. A good blanket, rough clothes, strong shoes, and a convenient knapsack, are absolute esentials; but don't burden yourself with needless things. In fact, while nothing is needed in the way of choice cravats and white kids, there should be careful regard to the little things you will need but cannot buy in the woods, even to a stout-bladed jack-knife.

It is impossible, and useless to attempt, to describe particular spots, which would tempt a "camping-out" party to prefer. They are numbered by thousands. If you would have large game on land, and salmon in the waters, a location must be chosen in the more wild and rugged regions of our remote borders; and in the right season, — say, in early May. Should a more quiet and subdued locality be preferred, you may push for the mountain sides and slopes of Pennsylvania or of Virginia. No more attractive beauties of nature invite the tourists of our land, than await those who may seek the elevated portions of "Old Virginny."

Prince Edward's Island is also unsurpassed in natural charms, in healthfulness, in its sources for camping-out pleasures, and the broad hospitality of its rural population. In due time, a great summer pilgrimage will set towards that garden of the sea.

Nova Scotia abounds in novelties to our own people, and in its fine lakes, filled with the most eager and gamey of trout.

The solitudes of New Brunswick, so strangely overlooked by travellers and writers, possess some of the loveliest as well as the grandest and most romantic attractions to be found on any portion of our continent This picturesque region also will soon, no doubt, be opened by pleasure hunters and the writers of many books.

Northern Maine about Moosehead and the Rangeley Lakes, the hills and streams of Vermont, a great and grand region lying between the White Mountains and Canada, a lovely land around the head waters of the Connecticut River, not forgetting Mount Desert nor the Adirondacks, — these are some of the leading areas of our Northern climate, where camping out may be enjoyed, in all its delicious and inspiring fulness.

This is all that space will permit in this work, for remarks upon "camping out." As yet it is only here and there that the camping-out party is to be found, in the warm months. The attention of vacation takers has not been turned to this best of all modes of seeking one's comfort and ease, to the degree required to make it popular and general. But it cannot be commended too earnestly, nor pressed too persistently upon public notice. It is not absolutely required that the party camping out shall locate in a place remote from all civilization. On the contrary, a vast number of our more popular summer resorts and towns offer most inviting spots for a camp (see cut) to which the belles would delight to ramble, and where primitive hospitality can be liberally dispensed, even when young bucks of fashion may be compelled to act the parts of Bridget the cook, and Mary the maid of all work. It is a matter of surprise that this charming way to diversify the individual and family trip is not more generally remembered and practised. Let the reader, as he decides whither his summer flight shall be, ponder well this idea of "Camping Out."

Harbor and Coastwise Excursions. — One of the most delightful yet economical sources of summer enjoyment is the harbor excursion. From each of our great maritime cities, boats conveniently arranged leave daily for some of the most popular resorts. From Washington they sail down the Potomac to Mount Vernon; from Baltimore to the beautiful water retreats in the vicinity; from New York up the North and East Rivers, to Staten Island, and Harlem; from Boston to Nantasket Beach, Long Island, Gloucester, and Nahant. Indeed, every large town with a harbor front has its pleasant resorts; and the stranger has only to look in the daily papers for particulars.

Again: if the tourist would consult comfort and economy, if he would take sleep and rest while passing familiar or uninteresting sections of the country, he can frequently give diversity to his travels by an occasional trip on a coastwise steamer. In going east from Boston, the daily steamboat line to Portland, the "Star of the East" up the Kennebeck, "Sanford's Independent Line" up the Penobscot, the "Inside Line" from Portland to Mount Desert and Bangor, and the Halifax boats, are all first-class, and deserving the notice of tourists. The New York boats are described elsewhere.

NORTH CONWAY, N.H.

When the days begin to lengthen, and the sun runs high in the heavens; when the short nights fail to cool the heated streets of a dusty city, and man feels that he must have respite from the care and excitements of business; when the mother rises in the morning unrefreshed,

CONWAY ELMS.

and the children grow languid for a change; when, finally, the family council decide that a few weeks' vacation must be spent in the country, — no place can be found where the cool mountain air blows fresher, where the crystal streams flow purer, or where Nature wears a lovelier garb, than at *North Conway*. Since the early settlement of the country, the praises of Conway's rich meadows have been sung. To-day her broad-sweeping elms and luxuriant gardens indicate the strength of their rich alluvial soil.

Conway Valley forms the great natural thoroughfare to the White Mountain region, over which *Kiarsarge* — her favorite mountain — stands sentinel. There is no place in New England combining more interesting and enjoyable features than North Conway. The means of communication, by the "Eastern" and "Portland and Ogdensburg" Railroads, cannot be excelled, in the easy transits or luxuriant comforts they afford. The wide-spread popularity of this summer resort attracts thousands of visitors here annually; where they readily obtain ample accommodations, from the quiet farm, the pleasant and economical boarding-house, to the magnificent summer hotel.

KIARSARGE HOUSE,
North Conway, N.H.

"**The Kiarsarge**" is a new and elegant hotel, built with a special regard to the wants of pleasure travel, containing over two hundred rooms, and has ample accommodation for three hundred guests. It is located in the very heart of the village, commanding one of the grandest and most extensive views of mountain scenery to be found in New England. Extending around the hotel is a broad covered piazza, which connects with a plank walk leading to the depot, affording a fine promenade of over one thousand feet. This promenade commands, in one grand sweep, the entire White Mountain range, with Mount Washington in the centre, showing Tip-Top House plainly in view. Mount Kiarsarge, the Mote Mountains, the White Horse, and Humphrey's Ledges are embraced in the scene; while in the immediate foreground we have the lovely "Meadows," which have long been celebrated, with their tall and gracefully sweeping elms, combining one of the finest views in the country.

The interior of "The Kiarsarge" is fitted up with every modern improvement; and the house throughout is furnished with especial reference to the comfort and convenience of guests. On the first floor is the office, parlor, reception-room, dining-hall, gentlemen's reading-room, billiard-hall, barber-shop, and wash-rooms. The rotunda, in the centre of the building, is forty feet square, and well lighted, with an entrance from the front and rear, affording such perfect ventilation, that in the warmest day one is here sure of a cool retreat. The parlor is an elegant room, forty by sixty; and here, during the season, one may listen for six nights in the week to the best concert and dancing music.

The dining-hall is a well-lighted and cheerful room, with a seating capacity for three hundred guests, commanding an admirable view of the White Mountain groups.

All the public rooms, including the ladies' parlor, on the second story, have been richly frescoed. The house is lighted with gas; and, to meet the increasing autumn patronage, steam has been introduced into the entire lower story, thus insuring a uniform temperature for the cool days of early autumn. On the second, third, and fourth stories are the sleeping-rooms, arranged singly and in suites. They are high, airy, and thoroughly ventilated; and all have bells connecting with the office.

The beds consist of the best springs and hair mattresses.

The table, as heretofore, will be supplied with all the luxuries of the season, and served in the best manner.

Passengers from Boston *via* Portland, over the Eastern, Boston, and Maine Railroad, or by boat, will take the cars of the Portland and Ogdensburg Railroad, which connect twice a day with trains from Boston.

Passengers from New York and the West, *via* Boston, can connect with the above routes; *via* Concord, over the Boston, Concord, and Montreal Railroad, leave the cars at Weir's, and take the boat across the lake for Centre Harbor; and from there stages run to West Ossipee, connecting with trains for North Conway.

This celebrated region has long been famous as a summer resort, but was never more popular than at this time. It is easily reached from all points, and is not only a desirable place to remain weeks, or even months, but is also the grandest entrance to the White Mountains. "From no other locality can they be approached to so good advantage; and by no other route can so much of interest be seen with so little travel and expense."

Stage and railroad connections are made twice each day with the Crawford and Fabyan Houses and Mount Washington Railway, and the same with the Glen House, and carriage-road up Mount Washington.

MT. KIARSARGE FROM NORTH CONWAY.

North Conway has an additional advantage, wholly and peculiarly her own. She has a mountain, — Mount Kiarsarge, — which forms an admirable objective point for her visitors. It is only two miles distant, and three more to its summit; yet the prospect from it combines some of the finest panoramic scenery in New England. A small hotel on its crest affords refreshments and shelter for those who desire.

The climate of North Conway is free from mists and fogs; and with its pure air, and dry and invigorating atmosphere, it is one of the most desirable points in the whole White Mountains for those who may be seeking health or pleasure. "And then the sunsets of North Conway! Coleridge asked Mont Blanc if he had 'a charm to stay the morning star in his steep course.' It is time for some poet to put the question to those bewitching elm-sprinkled acres that border the Saco, by what sorcery they evoke, evening after evening, upon the heavens that watch them, such lavish and Italian bloom. Nay, it is not Italian: for the basis of its beauty is pure blue; and the skies of Italy are not nearly so clear as those of New England. One sees more clear sky in eight summer weeks in Conway, probably, than in the compass of an Italian year."

North Conway is not only noted for the beauty of its scenery in the spring and summer months, but later in the season the bright tints of its autumn foliage make it more lovely than ever; and nowhere can the magnificence of the autumnal forest scenery of New England be seen to better advantage than on her hills and mountains.

DIANA'S BATHS.

Few localities are better or more favorably known to the "artist world" than North Conway. The variety of the scenery is particularly noticeable; while it possesses some of the broadest landscape and mountain views, it is celebrated for the beauty and artistic value of its choice "bits."

POPULAR RESORTS. — Diana's Baths, Ledges, Echo Lake, and Cathedral, 3 miles. These places are across the Saco River, and may be visited in one excursion, the drive occupying about three hours.

Kiarsarge Mountain. Carriages to base of mountain, 2 miles; saddle horse to summit, 3 miles. Total, 5 miles.

Goodrich Falls, 7 miles; Jackson Falls, 9 miles. This is a pleasant afternoon excursion; and both places may be visited at the same time.

Jockey Cap, 11 miles; Lovell's Pond, 13 miles. Both visited in half a day's excursion.

Chocorua Lake and Mountain, 18 miles.

Glen Ellis Falls, 16 miles; Swift River Falls, 18 miles.

Thorn Hill, 8 miles. A charming afternoon drive, with grand views of the mountains.

Carter's Notch, 12 miles; Sligo, 13 miles; Humphrey's Ledges, 11 miles; Potter's Farm, 12 miles; Thompson Falls, 6 miles; Artist Fall, 1 mile; Washington Bowlder, 7 miles; Bartlett Bowlder, 6 miles.

BOSTON AND MAINE RAILROAD.

This is one of the most popular routes of summer travel in New England. It not only forms a through line between Boston and Maine, as its name suggests, but, through its connections, leads to Canada, the Provinces, and directly to the picturesque lake and mountain regions of New Hampshire. The equipments of this road are unrivalled, both in the use of all modern improvements for safety, and in the taste displayed in their manufacture.

This route possesses the advantage of leaving Boston from the heart of the city. Its depot, in Haymarket Square, at the head of Washington Street, is more central than that of any other road. The line is located through a section of the country possessing unusual interest. The trains, which leave Boston in a northerly direction, cross the Charles River, and, passing through *Charlestown*, almost under the shadow of Bunker-Hill Monument, glide rapidly away through the suburbs which skirt the city in that direction. The stations at *Somerville*, *Malden*, *Melrose*, *Stoneham*, and *Greenwood* are quickly passed. These places are each beautiful in themselves, and by their constant communication with Boston are rendered particularly desirable for residences. From *Wakefield* a branch road leads to *Georgetown*, *Danvers*, and *Newburyport*. *Wakefield* is but ten miles from Boston, and is a thriving and beautiful town. *Reading*, *Wilmington*, *Ballardvale*, and *Andover* are next passed. The latter place is the seat of a theological seminary. The Salem and Lowell railroad intersects the Boston and Maine at *Wilmington Junction*. In one hour from the start the train reaches *Lawrence*, one of the most important cotton-manufacturing cities in the country. This city is located on the northern bank of the Merrimac River. Those desiring to stop here, or continue to *Manchester*, *Concord*, *Northern New Hampshire*, *Vermont*, or the *Canadas*, should take the rear cars, which are detached at South Lawrence, and continue to their destination. The main line follows the right bank of the Merrimac to *Bradford*, from which place another branch leads to *Georgetown* and *Newburyport*. The road crosses the river from *Bradford* to *Haverhill*. This small but tasteful city possesses few rivals, either in the thrift of its inhabitants, or in the picturesque beauty of its location. It is situated on the left bank of the Merrimac, which is to this place navigable for small steamers. The ground rises gradually from the river, affording to each successive tier of houses an admirable view of the surrounding country.

Three miles beyond Haverhill the train passes *Atkinson*, and enters *New Hampshire:* although the country for twenty miles, through the towns of *Plaistow*, *Newton*, and *East Kingston*, will hardly fulfil the traveller's expectations of New-Hampshire scenery. From *Newton* a " Branch "

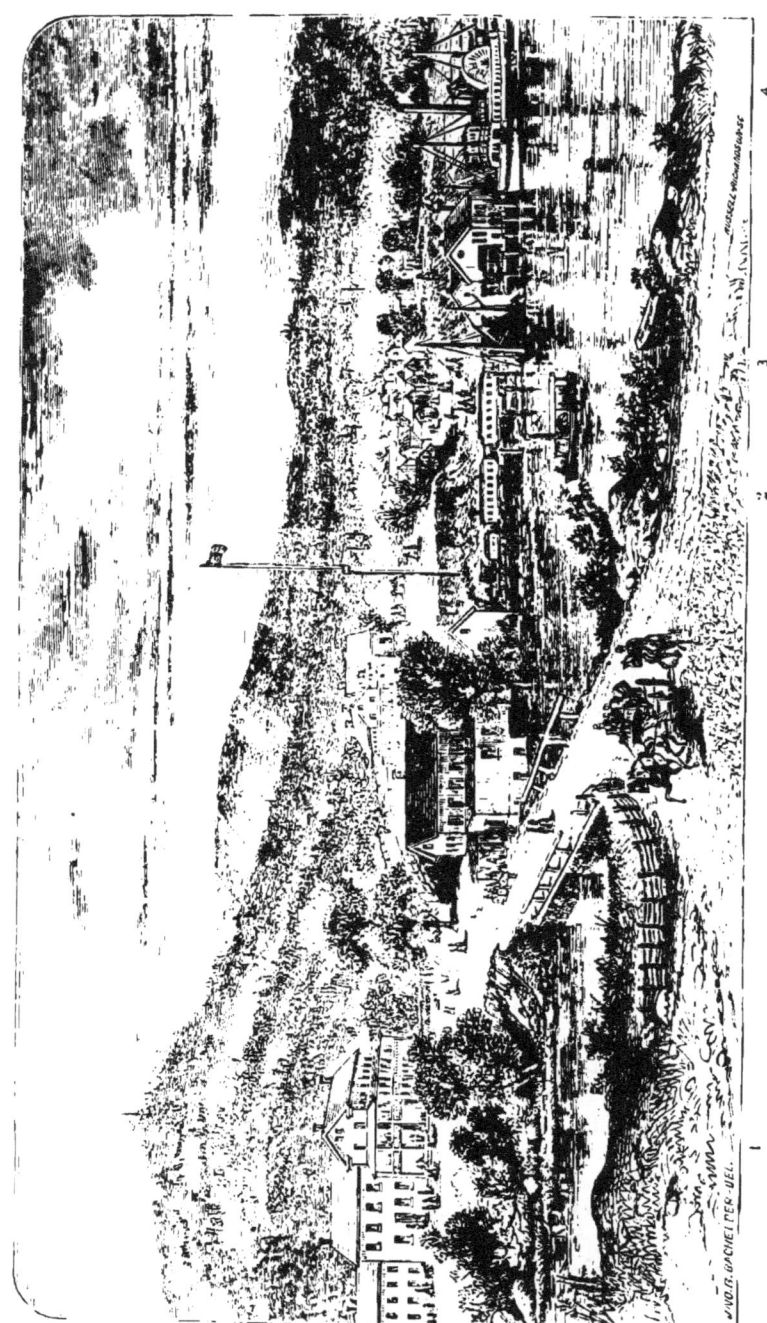

Engraved expressly for "Bachelder's Popular Resorts, and How to Reach Them."

ALTON BAY, N.H.

1. Bay View House.
2. Boston and Maine R.R.
3. Camp-Meeting Grounds.
4. Steamer "Mt. Washington."

leads to *West Amesbury*. *Exeter*, the next place of importance, is an unusually desirable town. The Phillips Academy, and the Robinson Female Seminary, two of the best schools in the State, have given a tone to society, the influence of which is at once felt by the visitor.

From this station a stage runs, during the summer months, to *Hampton Beach*, eight miles distant, although that resort can be more directly reached by rail.

At the Exeter Station will be found an excellent restaurant, where the train always waits full ten minutes. Beyond Exeter we pass *South New Market*, *New Market Junction*, and *New Market*. The villages are both pleasantly situated; while at the "Junction" connection is made with the Portsmouth and Concord Railroad, by which passengers can visit either of those cities and other points on the line. From New Market to Dover, through *Durham* and *Madbury*, the route passes through an agricultural region. *Dover* is a city of 10,000 inhabitants, located on the Cocheco River, and has a fine water-power. At this place the road divides; the main line continuing to *Portland*, while a "Branch" (the Dover and Winnepesaukee Railroad) extends to *Alton Bay*. This route has steadily increased in popularity until it is accounted one of the most desirable to *Lake Winnepesaukee* and the *White Mountains*. By it the lake is approached at the southern extremity; where close connection is made with the new and beautiful side-wheel steamer **Mount Washington,** Captain Wiggin, which sails its entire length (30 miles), stopping at all landings, and returning the same day, connecting with the last train for Boston.

Alton Bay, at the terminus of the railroad, is a quiet hamlet shut in by hills. The **Bay View House** is pleasantly and conveniently located, and affords, at reasonable cost, good accommodations to its guests. The mountain-drives in the neighborhood present many magnificent views of the lake and surrounding country, that to *Gilmanton* being particularly noticeable. Gilmanton is a quiet country town. Its surface is high rolling upland, with clear, exhilarating atmosphere, and pure water slightly impregnated with iron. It is one of the most healthful localities in the State; in evidence of which may be cited the unusual number of aged people among its inhabitants, some being over one hundred years. It has three villages; at the "Centre" is located that time-honored institution, Gilmanton Academy. The town covers a great extent of country, and has many beautiful lakelets and small ponds, well stocked with fish. Its quiet farms have become very popular as summer residences for families from the city. *Gilmanton Ironworks* is reached by the Boston and Maine Railroad to Alton. *Gilmanton Academy*, by the Boston, Concord, and Montreal Railroad to *Tilton*, and *Lower Gilmanton*, *via* Concord and Suncook Valley Railroads to *Pittsfield*, and thence by stages from each station.

Engraved expressly for "Bachelder's Popular Resorts, and How to Reach Them."

WOLFBORO', N.H.

1. Steamer "Mt. Washington."
2. Wolfboro' Mountain.
3. Steamer "Lady of the Lake."
4. Glendon House.
5. Bellevue Hotel.
6. Pavilion Hotel.

Ten miles from Alton Bay, at *Wolfboro'*, the steamer makes its first landing. *Wolfboro'* is built on land sloping to the water, and commands a fine view of the lake and the mountain-range beyond. The fame of this inland watering-place has long been known. There are three or four hotels: the **Glendon** and **Bellevue** standing at the water's edge; the **Pavilion** on higher land. There are also several private boarding-houses, affording ample accommodations to visitors. Connection is here made with the Wolfboro' Branch of the Eastern Railroad, leading to *North Conway* and the White Mountains.

GLENDON HOUSE, Wolfboro, N. H.

The *Glendon House* possesses several peculiar advantages, which suggest themselves to a person visiting Wolfboro'. It is located directly between the landing of the steamers "Mt. Washington" and "Lady of the Lake," and the station of the Eastern Railroad; and, being less than a stone's-throw from either, the arrival of the several trains and boats form a prolific source of amusement to guests. The house has been placed to give a water-prospect from every side, while the mountain views beyond add beauty and grandeur to the scenery. It has the further advantage of being new and newly furnished; and careful attention has been given to the drainage. A double veranda surrounds "The Glendon," affording delightful shade and fine promenades at all times. But one of its chief attractions is the peculiar construction of the roof, which, being flat, gives an unsurpassed opportunity to examine the surrounding country, and is a popular resort at the twilight of a summer's day.

From here the full grandeur of the surrounding mountain peaks is seen. *Copple-Crown*, that grand old mount, isolated and alone, rises in the south-east. It is but five miles away, over a pleasant road, which reaches far up its side. The view from its summit is magnificent, and will amply repay a visit. *Tumble-down Dick* is the name given to another peak in the neighborhood, probably from its one-sided appearance. Looking south-west, across the lake, the Guilford Mountains commence to rise from the water's edge; *Mt. Belknap* and *Gunstock* cutting sharply against the western sky. To the north they rise in grander forms: *Ossipee* Mountain, being nearest, holds a prominent position. The *Sandwich* Mountains beyond are decided in outline, and artistic in combination; but rising grandly and boldly above them all is *Mt. Chocorua*, 3,358 feet above the sea. This peak is so decided in outline and character, that it is never mistaken. Many other mountains cut the distant horizon; and their study forms a source of amusement to the tourist.

The *Ossipee Falls* are on a wild mountain torrent a few miles distant, and are becoming a source of much resort.

Nearly synonymous with the history of Wolfboro', as a popular resort, is the name of the **Pavilion** as a first-class hotel; and few houses in New Hampshire are better or more favorably known. Unlike many of its age, the Pavilion does not grow old, but continues to improve with the rapid growth of the village; which now supports two first-class hotels, and several others at less prices, but where the comforts of home can be had.

Each year adds to the improvements or embellishments of this house; while the shrubbery with which the extensive grounds were early planted now forms an unceasing source of comfort and delight, particularly to children in their amusements.

Since the close of the last pleasure season, it has been placed in perfect repair; commencing at the foundation and drainage, the plumbing and painting; in a word, the "Pavilion" has been rejuvenated, and, dressed in holiday attire, is ready to receive its numerous guests.

The house and grounds command an unobstructed view of the lake, its islands, and the mountain ranges beyond. Its lawn, embracing six acres, is well laid out, slopes gently down five hundred feet to the water's edge, where a fine wharf has been erected, and is maintained for the exclusive use of guests. Indeed, boating is one of the favorite amusements of the *habitués* of Wolfboro'.

This town has become a very popular summer home for the families of business men of Boston. By the convenient arrangement of trains and boats, the cars reach the city by ten o'clock in the morning, and return at 5, P.M., allowing a full day for business, and still chance to spend the night, morning, and evening at this charming resort.

1. Steamer "Lady of the Lake."
2. Steamer "Mt. Washington."
3. Senter House.
4. Moulton House.

Engraved expressly for "Batchelder's Popular Resorts, and How to Reach Them."

CENTRE HARBOR, N.H.

Wolfboro' has several churches and banks, and is withal a delightful place to spend the summer and autumn months.

Centre Harbor has become extensively known as a summer resort, and the **Senter House**, its principal hotel, as a pleasant, homelike place, where, by good fare and close attention to the comforts of his guests, its genial landlord has won a deserved popularity.

The house has been placed with special reference to the unrivalled prospect of the lake, which its situation commands. It has an unintercepted view for more than twenty miles. Here, seated under its broad verandas, shaded by magnificent elms, the visitor may watch the arrival and departure of the boats, the hurry and excitement of passengers, the going and coming of the stages, and the joy and exhilaration of the mountain parties leaving for or returning from **Red Hill**. The broad avenue which passes the house is shaded by a double row of elms, beyond which cultivated grounds slope gently down, two hundred yards, to the lake. The fine boat-houses and billiard and bowling saloons, which stand at the water's edge, are approached by walks ornamented by shrubs and flowers, and spanned by vine-clad arbors. Centre Harbor and its vicinity is noted for its good roads and delightful drives, one of the most popular of which is to **Red Hill**. Although this mountain rises to the height of 2000 feet, its ascent is not difficult. A four-mile drive over a country road brings the tourist to the base of the mountain, from which a good pedestrian can easily make the remaining two miles; or, for those who desire, trained saddle-horses are always to be had.

I will not volunteer a description of the view from Red Hill, preferring to give the opinion of one of America's most popular writers (Rev. Thomas Starr King). I will simply add, that the remarkable grandeur of the view is due to the fact that this famous spot is surrounded by the most noted mountain-peaks on this coast, while its base is bathed by the waters of a beautiful lake.

" The excursion to Red Hill is easily made in the afternoon, or between breakfast and dinner. Its unwooded peak is lifted to the height from which scenery looks most charming; and there is no point except this along the regular mountain route beneath which a lake is spread. But here Winnepesaukee stretches from its very foot; and its whole length is seen as far as the softly swelling hills that bound it on the southeast. Here is the place to study its borders, to admire the fleet of islands that ride at anchor on its bosom, — from little shallops to three-deckers, — and to enjoy the exquisite lines by which its bays are enfolded, in which its coves retreat, and with which its low capes cut the azure water, and hang over it an emerald fringe. And, if one can stay late in the afternoon as we have staid, and see the shadows thrown out from the islands and the trees, and the hues that flush the lake's surface as the sun declines, he obtains the most fascinating and enjoyable view which can be gained from any eminence that lies near the tourist's path."

A short walk back from the Senter House leads by gentle ascent to points of rare interest, commanding views of the surrounding country, and the lake, which, like an immense mirror, reflects the hills and islets for miles and miles away.

The time is not far distant when this desirable slope will be covered by summer residences: a spot so beautiful and accessible cannot long fail to attract public notice. It not only commands a grand landscape view, but every movement about the boats and hotels.

LAKE WINNEPESAUKEE, N.H.
From Centre Harbor.

Squam Lake is also one of the favorite spots to visit. The drive is but two or three miles over the hills, yet it is very pleasant; while the lake is a perfect gem of loveliness. Its serrated coast, its points and inlets, and its fine gravelly beaches washed by the purest waters, combine to make this a favorite resort; fishing excursions here are also frequent. Squam Lake is passed by the excursionist who drives from Centre Harbor to *Plymouth*. There are many other delightful drives in the vicinity, for the enjoyment of which ample accommodations are furnished at the hotels.

The Senter House is reached directly by three of the most popular lines of railroad in New England, viz., the Boston and Maine (already described), the Boston, Concord, and Montreal, and the Eastern to Wolfboro', where connection is made by boat to Centre Harbor.

SCENE ON LAKE WINNEPESAUKEE.

Stages leave, morning and noon, for *West Ossipee* (20 miles) viâ *Moultonboro'*, *Tamworth*, and *Sandwich*, where connection is made with the cars for *North Conway*, *Bartlett*, and the **White Mountains**; although tourists from Centre Harbor to the White Mountains are not confined to the stage, two other routes being open morning and evening, — viâ Steamer "Mt. Washington," and the Wolfboro' and Conway Branch, and the Boston, Concord, and Montreal Railroad viâ Steamer "Lady of the Lake."

Engraved expressly for "Batchelder's Popular Resorts, and How to Reach Them."

SACO FALLS, ME.

Boston and Maine Railroad.

The approach to Centre Harbor presents many features of unusual interest. The moving diorama, as the steamer threads its way among the islands, forms a perfect kaleidoscope of beauty. At every turn the landscape changes. Green hills, rich pastures, and quiet waters compose the view, beyond which the White Mountains tower in stately grandeur.

Resuming our route from *Dover* on the main line, the train will first stop at *Rollinsford*, from whence a Branch road leads to *Great Falls*, a thriving cotton-manufacturing town with a fine water-power, on the Salmon-Falls River. *Salmon Falls* is the next village. This is also a manufacturing place; the same river runs through the village, and is here crossed by a high bridge (see cut), beneath which the angry waters boil and tumble. The route of the Boston and Maine Railroad to this point has been inland. From here it leads again towards the sea, crossing the Eastern Railroad at *Berwick*, and continuing to *Wells*. This is the direct route to *Wells Beach*, which is but two miles from the depot. Coaches are run from every train by the hotel-proprietors.

ISLAND LEDGE HOTEL.

This house derives its name from its location, and from the ledge which breaks the incoming waves in its front. It is pleasantly situated, standing high, surrounded by a beautiful graded and highly cultivated lawn. The views are extensive, commanding over thirty miles of water horizon, from Cape Porpoise in the east, to Bald Head Cliff in the south. The inland prospect is unobstructed. The Wells River runs between the hotel and town; beyond all is an extensive landscape view.

The **Atlantic House** also possesses a good local reputation, and is pleasantly located at the southern end of the beach.

Kennebunk is the next regular station on the Boston and Maine Railroad

This is an old town, inhabited largely by retired merchants and seafaring men. The new watering-place and summer resort at *Cape Arundel, Kennebunkport,* is but three miles distant, connected by stage.

CAPE ARUNDEL.

Cape Arundel differs materially from any other resort on the coast. The sand-beach is short, though very good. It has several gravelly beaches, adapted to bathing; but its chief characteristic is a stern rock-bound shore, interspersed with those cavernous apertures into which the tide rushes with violence, often throwing the water to a great height. There is a good hotel of medium capacity, but well kept; a fine wharf, with admirable facilities for fishing and sailing; while the vicinity abounds in berries. Every thing is new, and to those pleased with that character of scenery is a pleasant retreat. The country from Kennebunk possesses little to interest the traveller until he reaches *Biddeford,* a city of rapid growth, an offshoot from *Saco,* the station on the opposite side of the river. Saco and Biddeford are manufacturing towns, located on the Saco River, which at this place has a fall of fifty-five feet, furnishing one of the finest water-powers in the State. The Boston and Maine Road crosses by a wrought-iron bridge immediately above the falls, of which a fine view may be had from the cars.

Saco Pool is a land-locked basin near the mouth of the river, nine miles below Saco and Biddeford, and as a summer resort possesses a fine local reputation. Several hotels are open for the season. It is reached by a small steamer from the landing at Biddeford.

From Saco the cars bear away to *Old Orchard Beach,* passing, at places, almost within the spray of the surf, and depositing tourists at the door of the hotels. *Old Orchard* has one of the finest sand-beaches on the coast.

Engraved expressly for Bachelder's "Popular Resorts, and How to Reach Them."

SALMON FALLS, N.H.

It is nine miles long, very hard, and presents admirable facilities for driving and bathing. From Old Orchard to *Portland*, eleven miles, the scenery is uninteresting, though the old watering-place at *Scarborough* is but a short distance off the road, and still attracts its favorite visitors.

Engraved expressly for Bachelder's " Popular Resorts, and How to Reach Them."

OLD ORCHARD BEACH.

1. Old Orchard House.
2. Ocean House.
3. Boston and Maine R. R.
4. Sea Shore House.
5. Gorman   "
6. Montreal   "
7. St. Cloud   "

Portland is a beautiful city, handsomely built, finely located on dry, commanding ground, and beautifully ornamented by shade-trees and public boulevards. It has superior hotels; and the suburbs present many interesting features. It has a deep, well-protected harbor. *Cape Elizabeth*, a bold, rock-bound coast on the southern side, is a place of considerable resort during the summer months.

Cooperstown. — "This popular resort is the county seat of Otsego County, N.Y., and is situated at the south end of Otsego Lake. It is one of the literary Meccas of America; for here was the home of J. Fenimore Cooper, and in these scenes he wrote those wonderful American stories, which the English-reading world have placed on a level of popularity with the undying fictions of Walter Scott. In his 'Deerslayer,' he describes the lake and surrounding hills. A late guide-book says,— 'The same points still exist which "Leather-Stocking" saw. There is the same beauty of verdure along the hills; and the sun still glints as brightly as then the ripples of the clear water.' The whole region is full of interest, because of the creations of Cooper's genius; and his romances have a new zest and beauty when read amid the scenes that inspired them. The surroundings of the lake are all beautiful; and the entire region is full of interest. In close proximity are several favorite resorts, accessible by a small steamer which runs on the lake, which is widely famed for its bass and pickerel fishing."

Trenton Falls. — "These remarkable curiosities are near the city of Utica, N.Y., on West Canada Creek, a tributary of the Mohawk River, and consist of a series of cascades, of unexcelled picturesqueness and beauty. The principal falls are five in number, and are named, successively, passing up the stream, Sherman Fall, High Fall, Mill-dam Fall, Alhambra Fall, and Rocky Heart. To appreciate them fully, the tourist should descend the bank, by stairway, to the rocky level at the bottom, and pass up along the left bank, on an irregular line of shelf-path, presenting little difficulty and no danger to the careful. The rock strata of the gorge cannot fail to excite admiration; and the unique collection of fossils and crystals, found in the neighborhood and kept on view at a hotel near the Falls, is an interesting subject for examination and study. From a point called the Rural Retreat, a splendid view of the High Fall, from above, can be had."

Straw's Point, N.H., is a group of private residences for summer life, as yet; but its many advantages for novelty and for health-seekers must soon raise the inevitable hotel in its vicinity, if not in its midst. It is but a half-mile from Rye Beach, and is reached from Boston by the "Eastern Railroad."

Rocky Point, R.I. — This famed resort is located on the shores of Narraganset Bay, and is passed by steamers from Providence to Newport. Its name suggests the wild, picturesque character of the scenery in the vicinity; yet "Rocky Point" is to-day more suggestive of clam-bakes and jolly times than any thing else. Excursion parties numbering thousands frequent it during the pleasure season.

Long Branch, "one of the most popular seaside resorts in America, is in Monmouth County, N.J. It was visited for health and recreation previous to 1812; and, soon after the termination of the war with Great Britain, hotels were opened for the accommodation of visitors. Still its magnitude is of recent growth; and the last fifteen years have done more for its development and improvement than the preceding fifty had accomplished. Its hotel accommodations are sufficient for fifteen thousand persons; yet each recurring season crowds them to their full capacity. Elegant and spacious cottages, owned and occupied by persons of distinction, line the principal avenues for long distances, some of them being surrounded with extensive grounds, highly ornamented and carefully kept.

"The beach at Long Branch is famous for its natural grandeur, as well as for its artificial attractions. It is an open bluff, rising some twenty feet or more above the tide-line, and extending a distance of five miles. Along this, the grand drive is constructed, and the principal hotels are erected. Here, during the season, showy and elegant equipages dash, in passing and repassing lines, while the verandas and porticoes are thronged with spectators. No view could well be more animated or attractive than this, with its life, gayety, and beauty, relieved by the wide and restless ocean, swelling and rolling in boundless perspective. Some of the inland drives are equally pleasant; and, in fact, the facilities everywhere offered for this exhilarating enjoyment may be ranked as one of the greatest attractions of the place.

"The Monmouth Park race-course is a few miles from Long Branch; and its annual meetings rank among the most popular in America. These take place during the 'season;' and the list of entries generally embraces all the famous horses on the turf. Nothing on this side of the Atlantic so nearly approaches an English 'Derby Day' as a sweepstake at Monmouth Park, when the multitudes from New York, Philadelphia, and all other adjacent cities and towns, pour out to witness the famed steeds contend for the championship."

The State of New Jersey fails to offer any natural wonders to attract its share of the sight-hunting and money-spending thousands, who afford a summer harvest for more favored States. But her beaches are among the finest, as elsewhere described. Doubtless spots of landscape exist worthy of some delay to those flitting birds of passage; but the Jerseyites make their summer jaunts to more attractive regions than they can find at home.

Greenwood Lake, N.Y., on the Erie Road, is another of those panoramic regions where novelties and rural charms are in unlimited diversity.

PENNSYLVANIA SCENERY.

The remarkable unfolding of the mineral resources of Pennsylvania during the last few years has developed some of the finest scenery on the continent. Deep gorges, bold precipices, and wild ravines, heretofore untrodden by human foot, now sparkle with the light of civilization. The screaming locomotive, guided by science, darts into the recesses of the mountains. Forests are levelled, valleys cleared, houses erected, cities reared, mines opened; and the very hills pour forth their hidden treasures.

This industrial research has opened up a new field for pleasure seekers. Probably no other locality on the continent has received a like increase of visitors. A few years ago the extensive coal region of Pennsylvania was comparatively unknown

LEHIGH VALLEY, MAUCH CHUNK, PENN
Looking South from Mt. Pisgah.

to the tourist; now thousands visit it annually, and return filled with admiration of the wild beauties it contains.

ROUTE OF APPROACH.

The direct route of approach to the coal regions of Pennsylvania from *New York*, *New England*, and the *Provinces* is by the **Central Railroad of New Jersey, its Branches and Connections**, and from *Philadelphia* by the **North Pennsylvania Railroad**.

This also is the most direct and the shortest route from New York to Easton, Allentown, Wilkes Barre, Reading, Harrisburg, Williamsport, the Oil Regions, Pittsburg, and the West, and is one of the very pleasantest to North Mountain and Watkins Glen (elsewhere described), and when connected will embrace one of the finest and most varied pleasure trips on the continent. It has also been opened as a through route from New York and Philadelphia to Saratoga, *via* Mauch Chunk, Wilkes Barre, Scranton, &c. (see description). We leave New York from the foot of Liberty Street, by the Central New Jersey Railroad Company's splendid ferry-boats to Jersey City, from which point our route by rail commences. The road leads at first in a general westerly direction, through a fine agricultural region, interspersed with thriving villages and elegant suburban residences. It is also a field replete with historic memories. *Washington's Rock*, the lofty crag from which that revered general was wont to study the position and note the movements of a foreign foe, is plainly visible from the cars.

At Hampton Junction the "Delaware, Lackawanna, and Western Railroad" connects for Delaware Water Gap, Scranton, Great Bend, and Binghamton.

At Phillipsburg, a picturesque town built on a bold bluff on the left bank of the Delaware River, opposite Easton, which it overlooks, the "Central Railroad" connects with the "Morris and Essex" and the "Belvidere" Railroads.

Easton is delightfully located at the confluence of the Lehigh and Delaware Rivers, the former leaping over a dam of twenty-one feet at this place. The town is approached by a magnificent bridge, one thousand feet long, and twenty-two feet high. It is constructed of wrought iron, resting on heavy cut-stone piers, and, including the rock-cuts in the vicinity, cost $650,000. Beneath this pass diagonally the Canal, "Belvidere Railroad," and foot-bridge; and under all rush the waters of the wild mountain torrent in its race to the sea.

This bridge connects the "Central New Jersey Railroad" with the "Lehigh and Susquehanna" Division on the north bank of the Lehigh, and with the "Lehigh Valley Railroad" on the south bank. By the latter route we continue to Bethlehem and Allentown. The picturesque beauty of the scenery increases from Easton, the cars following the graceful curves of the river, which is fringed and shaded by beautiful trees, while bold hills, clothed with luxuriant foliage, compose the background.

At Bethlehem the "North Pennsylvania Railroad," from Philadelphia, intersects with the "Lehigh Valley" and the "Lehigh and Susquehanna" Roads, contributing its quota of tourists from Philadelphia and the South. The "Lehigh and Lackawanna" Branch to Chapman's also leads from this point.

At Allentown the course of the river is from the north-west, up which the "Lehigh Valley" and "Lehigh and Susquehanna" Railroads extend, while connection is also made with the "Allentown Line;" which comprises the "East Pennsylvania Railroad," thirty-six miles from Allentown to Reading, and the "Lebanon Valley Railroad," fifty-four miles farther, to Harrisburg. The general course of this route is westerly. The scenery is unusually fine; and, differing entirely in character from the "New York and Allentown" section, it adds to the variety and pleasure of the tourist. At Harrisburg connection is made with trains on the "Pennsylvania and Northern Central Railroad," affording ample facilities to go North, South, or West.

THE LEHIGH VALLEY. — RESUMING FROM EASTON.

The "Lehigh and Susquehanna" Division of the "Central Railroad" connects at Easton, and, following the tortuous course of the Lehigh, winds its picturesque way through the mountains to the Susquehanna at Wilkes Barre, up which it follows to Pittston, and thence on the east bank of the Lackawanna to Scranton.

This is a main line, into which lead, from every direction, branches filled with trains burthened with the rich mineral products of this remarkable region. Coal is not the only product: iron, slate, &c., are manufactured in great abundance.

COAL VEIN.

Either of these is found in quantities sufficient to insure the wealth and prosperity of any section of the country. These industrial pursuits form an interesting source of information, as well as amusement, to the tourist. He often gazes in amazement upon the curious mechanism and ponderous implements employed. The enormous expenditures which have been made to develop and frequently to prepare to develop these enterprises, are a source of wonder. And when we realize that these features are but adjuncts to one of the finest combinations of natural scenery in America, we can better understand its growing popularity.

LEHIGH GAP,
(Looking Down).
Central Railroad of New Jersey.

"Soon after leaving Bethlehem, the mountains approach the bed of the stream, and at 'The Gap' fling themselves directly in its path, leaving no resource but to go through them, which it has accordingly done, cleaving the mountains from summit to base in its efforts to escape.

"It is not until the vicinity of Mauch Chunk is reached that the peculiar features of Lehigh Valley appear in perfection."

MAUCH CHUNK, PENN.
Mt. Pisgah and "Switch-back" Railway.

This wild, picturesque, and popular region is reached from New York and Philadelphia *via* Central New Jersey, North Pennsylvania, and connecting railroads.

The arrival of the morning trains at Mauch Chunk from New York and Philadelphia is at the hour of noon; and a hot dinner at the Mansion House is waiting to be served. This, to the frequenter of the Lehigh Valley, is the only announcement necessary; but to the stranger I will add that "The Mansion" has no superior in this region. It needs but one visit to insure a second. The cars of the "Central Railroad of New Jersey" stop at the door; and its location on the banks of the Lehigh, overhung by rugged mountains, all

MANSION HOUSE, MAUCH CHUNK, PENN.
Central Railroad of New Jersey

clothed with the fragrant rhododendron, is picturesque to the last degree.

The visitor to Mauch Chunk is advised to go without any pre-arranged plans. It is not a place to "do" by programme, as many tourists travel. It contains too much, has too many features of interest, so startling in their character, so grand in conception, and so beautiful in detail, that any previous plan of operations must in execution fall to nought. It is better to go untrammelled.

After finding yourself comfortably domiciled, go first to the veranda on the front of the house, and leisurely study the scene, an engraving of which is herewith submitted. It is truly a wonderful view, pleasing in art, yet far more so in nature. A glimpse of the entrance to the town shows through the narrow street to the left. Splendid residences cling

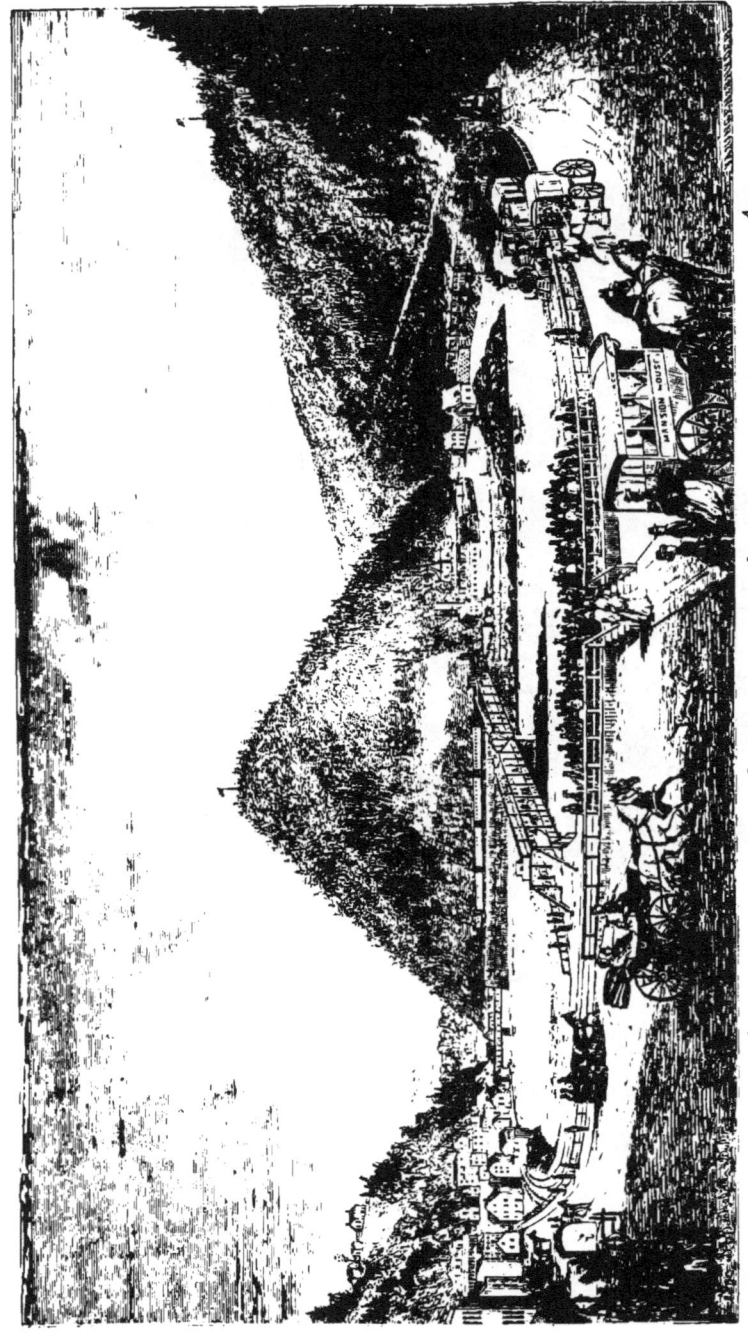

Engraved expressly for "Batchelder's Popular Resorts, and How to Reach Them."
VIEW FROM THE MANSION HOUSE, MAUCH CHUNK, PA.

1. East Mauch Chunk.
2. Bear Mountain.
3. Lehigh Valley R.R.
4. Lehigh & Susquehanna R.R.

to the hillside beyond, over which a few marble monuments indicate the village cemetery. Beyond this we take the cars for the "Switch-back" Railway. The "dam" in the left middle ground throws the water into

THE FLAGSTAFF.

the canal, whose boats, loaded with the "black diamonds" of this region, we have seen by the wayside. Immediately before the door is the platform of the "Central Railroad of New Jersey," where passengers are left and received from every train. The light iron bridge leads to the depot of the "Lehigh Valley Railroad," on the opposite side of the river. *Bear Mountain* is the central feature of the landscape.

But the mountain on the right receives the greatest homage from visitors. From the "Flagstaff" on its summit you get the view suggested by the above engraving, though vastly superior. It is too extensive, too grand, to receive justice from the artist's pencil. The topography of the whole country is spread out before you. It seems a moving diorama, through which you trace the serpentine windings of the Lehigh Valley, with its river, its railroads, and canals.

An excursion over the "Switch-back" Railroad will also be in order. Strictly speaking, the "Switch-back" has ceased to exist, and a *gravity* road has taken its place; but the name remains. The first improvement in the "Switch-back" Railroad — for conveying coal from the mines about Summit Hill, ten miles distant, to the boats of the "Coal Navigation Company" at Mauch Chunk — was by employing *gravity* one way, the grade being sufficient to insure this. Mules were taken down on the train to draw the cars back. This was subsequently improved by the construction of planes over the intervening elevations, Mt. Pisgah and Mt. Jefferson, up which the cars were drawn by stationary engines on their summits; the altitude thus gained being sufficient to turn the grade to Summit Hill, to which place the cars returned by their own gravity. This means of transportation answered well its purpose until the great demand for the anthracite coal of the "Lehigh" warranted the construction of a steam railroad, — the cutting of solid rocks asunder, and piercing the mountain barriers with tunnels.

MT. PISGAH PLANE.
"Switch-back" Railroad, Mauch Chunk, Penn.

The success of this last enterprise relieved the "Switch-back," or, more properly, "Gravity" Road; but the opening of this region at this time as a "popular resort" suggested the use of the "Switch-back"

Engraved expressly for "Bachelder's Popular Resorts, and How to Reach Them."

ONOKO STATION, MAUCH CHUNK, PA.

1. Moyer's Rock.
2. Central R.R. of New Jersey.
3. Lehigh Valley R.R.
4. Glen Onoko.

as a pleasure route for excursionists. Passenger cars have been substituted; and the same powerful machinery used for coal-cars is now applied to the light pleasure traffic. Carriages from the depots and the hotels take passengers to the base of Mt. Pisgah, though it is but a short distance for those who prefer to walk; and the fine scenery will repay the effort. The *plane* of Mt. Pisgah rises one foot in three for 2,322 feet. The cars are drawn up by a stationary engine on the top, connecting with an iron band six and one-half inches wide, which runs over a drum eighteen feet in diameter. The passenger car is followed by a *safety car*, supplied with a long iron bar following in a "ratchet," which, in case of breakage of engine or bands, securely holds the cars against accident; and its efficiency may be judged by the fact that there has never yet been an accident. On reaching the summit of Mt. Pisgah, the car starts by its own gravity down the opposite grade. Its course is gradual, following the tortuous sinuosities of the surface; now glancing under the shade of broad-spreading trees, for a moment refreshing all with their cooling shade; anon skirting the brink of a beetling crag, unfolding glimpses of the changing scenes below. Now we glide along the mountain side, and skim through the valleys, clearing at a bound the noisy streams which foam and boil far down among the rocks.

The ride is exhilarating beyond description. Without motive power, we seem to *fly through the air*. The winter coasting which delighted our childhood days tames in comparison.

The car is under the complete control of the brakemen. It would acquire a speed of forty-five miles an hour, but is kept at eighteen. Six miles our downward course is held, to the base of *Mt. Jefferson*, up which we are drawn as before, and again descend a single mile to *Summit Hill*, where a half-hour's stay is made. This is a mining hamlet, whose chief attraction to the tourist is the "Burning Mine," which has been on fire since 1832. The homeward ride is pleasant: we have no more *planes* to rise; our altitude is sufficient to give the grade, down which we glide nine miles to the point of starting. The pleasure of the party increases; familiarity with the scene has banished the fear of fancied dangers; and all return feeling that they have received an unusual amount of satisfaction for a dollar; and not unfrequently repeat it the next day.

It would seem that enough objects of interest about Mauch Chunk have already been described to insure its popularity; but the most beautiful feature remains.— **Glen Onoko.** Two miles above the village this fascinating spot is located. Cars by the "Central Railroad of New Jersey," and "Lehigh Valley Railroad," make several trips daily. It consists of a depression in the mountain, from which a fiery stream springs a thousand feet by successive leaps to the valley below, forming among the rocks and precipices a rare combination of waterfalls and cascades, which are clothed with deep evergreen foliage, and ornamented by the bright flowers of the rhododendron. At much time and expense a good path, stairways, and rustic bridges have been constructed, to facilitate the visitor. The accompanying "cut" of Onoko Station will convey a good idea of the locality, which is known to boatmen as the "Turn-Hole," from the "eddy" in the river formed by the current. The bluff on the left, through which the "Lehigh and Susquehanna" Division of the "Central Railroad of New Jersey" passes by tunnel, is properly known as **Moyer's Rock,** and possesses a traditional interest. The story is told in this wise: During the early settlement of the country, a noted hunter and Indian-fighter, living in Mahoning Valley, four miles south, who had hitherto eluded all attempts at capture, was surrounded, taken prisoner, and disarmed, by five Indian warriors, and left on the summit of this rock for security, guarded by two of their number, while the others hunted for game. Moyer was sorely perplexed. To fight alone two armed Indians was not to be thought of; and long he pondered. Suddenly starting, he listened intently, then relaxed into his former quiet. The Indians watched him unmoved. Again he started; and, creeping to the very brink, throwing into his countenance all the interest he could command, he gazed intently down. The ruse succeeded: overcome by curiosity, the Indians unguardedly moved to his side, and sought to discover the source of interest; when, with the spring of the tiger, he seized and dashed them to the rocks below.

The visitor to Glen Onoko should be well shod and suitably clothed, the refreshing coolness of the atmosphere rendering an extra "wrap" acceptable. The successive cascades, waterfalls, and other objects of interest, at Glen Onoko have each received appropriate names, and are worthy an individual description; but there are so many other interesting features of this picturesque region which demand a passing notice, that we must leave details to local guides.

Mauch Chunk is not, as many suppose, a mining town, but is, rather, the great coal-depot or shipping-mart of the Lehigh Valley. The production of coal is a subject of growing interest to the people of America; and, although it is not within the province of this volume to enter into a detailed description of the manner of working a coal-mine, yet a few lines for the benefit of those who would like to investigate the subject while in this region will be in place. The coal is found in veins of various thickness, and differently situated,— sometimes level, sometimes curved, often at an angle, and occasionally cropping out at the surface, from which the entrance is made. The experienced geologist can predict with approximate correctness the location of a vein of coal, and estimate the thickness of the overlying strata which must be pierced to reach it.

Sometimes these tunnels enter at the upturned edge of the vein, and

COAL BREAKER.

MINE.

descend with its inclination, and are termed *slopes*. These apertures are generally about eleven feet wide by seven feet high, and contain two railways, — one for the descending and one for the ascending cars, — and a "pump way" (for the mine must be continually cleared by the most powerful pumps), and a travelling or "man way." The slopes vary in length, frequently descending to great depths, passing at times under towns and rivers. The longest slopes in the anthracite regions are at New Philadelphia, or Lewis Vein, 2,700 feet; and at Diamond Vein, which is from 2,800 to 3,000 feet; these are on an incline of about 45°. "Gangways" are turned off to the right and left; and in working the coal a "pillar" is left every few feet which sustains the overlying strata of rock, and prevents it falling in.

Within a distance of from two to five miles from the town of Wilkes Barre, through which this route leads us, there are worked over forty mines, producing in some cases 1,500 tons of coal daily from a single mine.

The "Nesquehoning Valley Branch Railroad" leads from Mauch Chunk, and, connecting with the "Catawissa Railroad," extends to Williamsport, a distance of ninety-two miles.

This route is noted for the wildness of its scenery, its deep ravines, and high bridges, and must eventually become very popular with the pleasure-seeker.

THE LEHIGH.
Looking North from Mount Pisgah, Mauch Chunk
Central Railroad of New Jersey.

From Mauch Chunk northward the Lehigh Valley is little better than a cañon enclosed between high mountain walls, at whose base the narrow stream tumbles and foams; its waters now displaying the rich amber hue which they have distilled from the roots and plants in the swamps around their source, now white from their encounter with rock or fall. High rocks hang directly overhead, and threaten to fall at any moment upon the trains which constantly roll beneath: branches wave, and flowers blossom on the hillside, so close to the railroad track that the passengers can almost reach them without leaving their seats. Here and there a miniature waterfall springs from the mountain top, and glances, a ribbon of foam and spray, to the river at its foot; and at frequent intervals ravines cut in the mountain side present a confusion of rocks and wood and water to the eye of the traveller as he flashes by. Traced back a little from their mouths, these glens often show a wealth of beauty, a succession of snowy cascades, transparent pools, and romantic nooks, which are an ever fresh surprise to the explorer.

At Penn Haven, seven miles above Mauch Chunk, the "Lehigh Valley Railroad" connects with the "Mahanoy, Beaver Meadow, and Hazelton" Branches. The "Lehigh Valley" here crosses the river, and runs on the east bank to White Haven.

Fifty years ago this whole valley was a wilderness, with one narrow wagon-road crawling at the base of the hills beside a mountain torrent which defied all attempts to navigate it. Now the mountain walls make room for two railroads and a canal; but the tawny waters of the stream are nearly as free as ever. Here and there, indeed, a curb restrains them; and once an elaborate system of dams and locks tamed the wild river, and made it from Mauch Chunk to White Haven a succession of deep and tranquil pools. "But one day in 1862 the waters rose in their might. Every dam was broken, every restraint swept away; and from White Haven to Mauch Chunk the stream ran free once more. The memory of that fearful day is still fresh in the minds of the dwellers of the valley; and the bed of the torrent is still strewn with the wrecks that went down before its wrath." . . .

Nescopec Junction is a place of little importance; but the "Nescopec Branch Railroad" leads nine miles into a valley filled with wild and picturesque scenery.

This whole region is strange to the visitor. The valleys are deep, the precipices are bold and high, and the mountains steep. Even the waters rush with greater violence than in tamer countries. But the public will soon understand this scenery better. The artists, the pioneers of pleasure travel, have already heard of it, and each year visit it in increasing numbers. Soon the tide will set up this valley, hotels will be in demand to meet it, and the *press* will herald its praises.

Persons residing in our large cities hardly realize how quickly and for how small a sum these romantic places can be enjoyed. The morning train from New York or Philadelphia takes you to Mauch Chunk in season for dinner,—dinner steaming hot at the Mansion House. The "Switch-back" and Glen Onoko can be visited in season to return at night.

The subjoined description of the Nescopec region is from "Lippincott's Magazine:" —

"We walked about a half-mile along a wood-road, struck into a foot-

PROSPECT ROCK.
Nescopec Valley.

path, and followed it a hundred yards or so, and without warning walked out on a flat rock, from which we could at first see nothing but fog, up, down, or around. It was a misty morning; but we made out to understand that we were on the verge of a precipice, which fell sheer down into a tremendous abyss; and when the fog lifted we looked out upon miles and miles of valleys, partly cleared, but principally covered with primeval forests. We were on **Prospect Rock.**

"Presently our guide took us by a roundabout way to Cloud Point. This is a commanding projection on the other side of the glen; and here a still wider view — another, yet the same — lay before us. There is something indescribably grand in the solitude of this scene, — forests

CLOUD POINT, UPPER LEHIGH.

of giant trees lifting high their heads, in places, where growths for thousands of years have stood before, through which peer rough-visaged rocks which the hand of Time has failed to smooth. We gazed with delight on the beautiful landscape, then descended into Glen Thomas, a gem of scenic loveliness; fresh in its pristine beauty and grandeur.

"Our visit was made on the first of May. We found here miniature glaciers, formed by the water falling over the rocks, the ice three feet and more in thickness; while not a hundred yards away May-flowers were blooming in fragrant abundance. This region is filled with an untold wealth for the artist and lover of nature." And the time is not far distant when the travelling public, wearied by oft-repeated visits to old resorts, will demand the opening of these fresh and charming scenes.

From White Haven to the "Summit," on the main line, the landscape is more tame; the soil is poor; and the trees present that stunted appearance usual at high latitudes. But this brief respite tends to make the startling scenery through which the road soon passes even more effective. Having passed the crest of Wilkes Barre Mountain, the train glides rapidly down the opposite grade, and soon enters that wonderful gorge known as **Solomon's Gap**, the scene of the annexed engraving. This is the head of a system of *planes* by which loaded cars from the coal-fields below are raised by the Company of the Central Railroad of New Jersey.

We get here the first glimpse of "Wyoming Valley," which we are approaching at right angles. The Susquehanna can be seen in the valley, beyond which ranges of mountains rise in the blue distance. In altitude we are far, far above the Wyoming Valley; and the construction of the road by which it was reached was a rare feat of engineering skill. It is but three miles in an air-line to the small village of *Ashley*, seen below; yet, to overcome the grade, for eighteen miles the cars glance along the mountain sides, following in its zigzag course its varied irregularities.

GLEN THOMAS.

SOLOMON'S GAP.

1. Lehigh Valley Railroad.
2. Susquehanna.
3. Ashley.
4. Stationary Engine and Railroad "Flane"

We enter the gorge, and turn to the right, while across the valley can be seen the line of the "Lehigh Valley" Road, which, having kept us company from Bethlehem, now turns around the point to the left, to meet us twenty minutes later at the town below. The view from a half-mile below Solomon's Gap is remarkable. (See engraving.) Its composition varies so decidedly from any witnessed in the Lehigh Valley, that it always awakens feelings of surprise and awe. Here, surrounded by scenes of the wildest grandeur, the beautiful Wyoming Valley bursts like a flood of light suddenly upon you. The train glides smoothly on, the scene unfolds, and we are soon at *Ashley*, near the foot of the mountain.

From Ashley, ninety miles from Easton, the "Nanticote Branch Railroad" extends twelve miles to Nanticote, on the Susquehanna River. Wilkes Barre, ninety-nine miles from Easton, is located in Luzerne County, in the Valley of Wyoming, on the north branch of the Susquehanna. At this place visitors to the "North Mountain House" change to the "Lackawanna and Bloomsburg" Road; but it will be better to spend the night at Wilkes Barre. Fortunately they will find at the "Wyoming Valley Hotel" a house replete with everything necessary for the comfort of guests. It is pleasantly located on the banks of the Susquehanna, of which it commands some charming views.

The town of Wilkes Barre possesses historical associations of rare interest; its tragic deeds have oft been the theme of the historian's pen and the poet's muse. It is also a well-built town, and its surroundings are pleasant; and it will, withal, prove an interesting place of sojourn for tourists.

From Pittston, nine miles above Wilkes Barre, the road leaves the Susquehanna, and follows the course of the Lackawanna twelve miles, through Scranton to Green Ridge, where it connects with the "Delaware and Hudson Railroad" for Cooperstown, Sharon, and Saratoga Springs, Albany, Lake George, Lake Champlain, Montreal, &c.

"From New York and Philadelphia, the tourist to Saratoga, Watkins Glen, Niagara Falls, and the West is, by this route, transported through a wild and picturesque region, comparatively unknown to tourists. Much of the scenery is unlike that of any other section of the country; and, if only to gain a knowledge of the operation of the mammoth collieries of Pennsylvania, which have been scarcely alluded to in this article, it will amply repay an excursion on the 'Central Railroad of New Jersey,' its connections and branches."

Doubling Gap White Sulphur Springs. — "These springs are situated in, and take their name from, a gap formed by the doubling of the Kittatinny Mountains, about thirty miles south-west of Harrisburg, Penn., and seven miles from Newville, in the great Cumberland Valley. The waters, which flow from two springs, — one sulphurous and the other chalybeate, — contain valuable remedial properties, recommended by high medical authority, for various diseases. They have long been frequented by visitors, and deservedly enjoy a high degree of popularity. Located on the verge of one of the most extensive and beautiful valleys in the United States, where the air is remarkably pure, and the adjacent mountains unsurpassed for picturesque attractiveness, they present many charms, aside from their healing and rejuvenating waters. There are several other summer resorts accessible by the Cumberland Valley Railroad, such as the **York Springs**, four miles from Carlisle, and the **Mt. Holly Springs**, near the station of the same name. This entire region, in fact, is unsurpassed in natural beauty and historic interest; and no more delightful route could be selected for a summer journey than the Cumberland Valley, from the Susquehanna to the Potomac."

Alexandria Bay. — "This American port, on the St. Lawrence, is built upon a massive pile of rocks, and occupies a romantic and highly picturesque situation. Some two or three miles below the village is a position from which one hundred islands can be seen at one view. It is in Jefferson County, N.Y., in immediate contiguity to the '**Thousand Islands**,' which stretch themselves along the centre of the St. Lawrence River for a distance of forty miles below the termination of Lake Ontario. The steamboat ride from Cape Vincent to Alexandria Bay affords an excellent view of these islands, which are said to number between seventeen hundred and eighteen hundred. The river is about twelve miles wide, but is so closely studded with islands of all shapes and sizes, ranging from an acre to ten miles in length, that there really seems at times a difficulty in treading a channel through them. The water of the St. Lawrence is here of a bright green color, and beautifully clear. The islands are nearly all rocky, and thickly wooded; and the water in places so deep that the steamers could easily run within a few feet of some of the cliffs. Fishing and gunning among the islands are extremely good; and the region is much frequented by sportsmen, as well as by tourists in search of Nature's wonders and beauties. The Rapids of the St. Lawrence are reached a short distance below Alexandria Bay."

Salem, Mass., was once famous for its witches, and is now notable for wealth and refinement. It also possessed an extensive East India trade, which has been largely absorbed by Boston. It is reached by the "Eastern Road," and by rail from Lowell.

CAPE MAY.

This old, established, and most justly celebrated watering-place is situated at the extreme southern point of New Jersey, on a narrow peninsula extending a distance of ten miles, bounded by the waters of the Atlantic Ocean on one side, and the Delaware Bay on the other.

For more than half a century it has been the resort of persons seeking health and pleasure during the heated term of the summer months.

The perfect safety of the surf-bathing, and the firmness of its broad, even, and unbroken beach, are unequalled at any other seaside resort.

The difficulty in reaching *Cape May* prevented for many years the rapid improvements its admirable location seemed to warrant, until the **West-Jersey Railroad Company,** appreciating the immense advantages to be gained, have from time to time extended their lines, and in 1863 opened an all-rail route from Philadelphia.

Pleasure tourists, at once becoming acquainted with the facilities thus afforded, flocked to the Cape. Property increased in value; handsome and costly cottages were erected, large and commodious hotels built, novelties introduced; and great improvements were manifest.

The Railroad Company did not confine its efforts merely to building the road, but aided generously with its capital, not only individual enterprises, but those to develop the natural advantages of the place.

It now became the resort for the *élite* and fashionables of Baltimore, Washington, Pittsburg, and Philadelphia; and, among its many regular sojourners, Chicago, St. Louis, New Orleans, and San Francisco have their representatives.

The hotels at this most popular watering-place are conducted in every manner equal to the principal hotels of our largest cities: the leading houses, the "*Stockton,*" "*Congress Hall,*" and "*Columbia,*" each accommodating comfortably from one thousand to twelve hundred guests.

The Stockton Hotel, under the management of Charles Duffy, Esq., of the Continental Hotel, Philadelphia, is without doubt the most attractive and commodious house to be found at any of our seaside resorts; and, as a combination of mechanical and architectural beauty, it cannot be surpassed.

It is situated within seventy feet of the surf, directly facing the ocean, with a frontage of two hundred and ninety-three feet and a depth of three hundred and ninety-four feet, the wings on either side being fifty feet wide. The porticos are fourteen hundred feet long and twenty feet wide; forming a grand unbroken promenade, covered by an immense roof supported by majestic, towering pillars, sixty feet in height.

The Main Entrance Hall, or Rotunda — in which are situated the Office, and stairway of massive and handsome black-walnut — is one hundred feet long by fifty feet wide, forming a beautiful colonnade, separating the Office from the principal stairway.

The capacious Dining Hall, immediately adjoining the Rotunda, is capable of seating twelve hundred persons, it having a depth of two hundred and eighty feet, and width of sixty feet; while the high windows, opening from ceiling to floor, directly facing the ocean, admit at all times an invigorating sea-breeze.

The principal Parlor, fifty feet square, is situated at the extreme southern end, next the ocean, and is most elegantly furnished with heavy, elaborately carved, and handsome black-walnut furniture, lace curtains, mirrors extending from floor to ceiling, a Steinway Grand Piano, &c.

Reception Rooms, Drawing Rooms, Private Parlors, Reading

PHILADELPHIA TO CAPE MAY.

Rooms, Restaurants, &c., all furnished in the same gorgeous style, occupy the remainder of the ground floor. The building is four stories in height. The second, third, and fourth floors are divided into suites of rooms, and single sleeping-apartments.

The same exquisite taste displayed in the parlor furniture is perceptible in the furnishing of every room in the hotel; and — what is of rare occurrence in hotels — a magnificent large wardrobe can be found in every sleeping-apartment of this vast edifice.

An improved steam elevator carries guests from the main hall to each floor.

The Hotel has over eight hundred bath-houses for the accommodation of its guests.

It requires a constant force of over four hundred employés to thor-

STOCKTON HALL, CAPE MAY, N.J.

oughly manage the workings of this mammoth establishment; and, during the months of July and August of 1873, over thirty-five thousand guests were accommodated, aside from the transient daily business.

The appearance of the "Stockton," rising high above all other buildings of the Cape, together with its close proximity to the sea, is grand, majestic, and imposing; and from its large and airy rooms a splendid view, for miles, of the ocean, bay, and adjacent country, is presented.

A fine Band of Music, consisting of some twenty-five performers, discourses choice selections of the popular operas and composers.

Cape May can be reached direct from New York and Philadelphia by rail, *viâ* the Pennsylvania and West-Jersey Railroads.

Palace-cars are run through from New York without change. Three express-trains are run daily from Philadelphia, the time being about two and one-half hours.

ATLANTIC CITY, N.J.

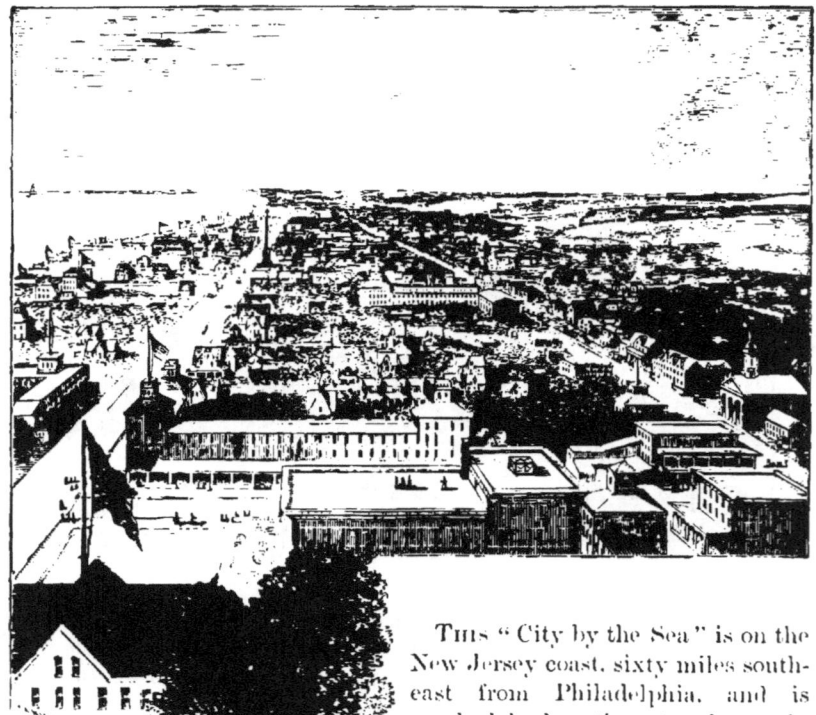

This "City by the Sea" is on the New Jersey coast, sixty miles southeast from Philadelphia, and is reached in less than two hours, in luxurious cars, by the **Camden and Atlantic Railroad.** This is the shortest route to the seashore by over twenty miles. Six trains daily, with two extras on Saturdays, carry their heavy burthens to this cool and healthful summer-resort. Woodruff parlor-cars are attached to all express-trains, which make but one stop on the way (at Hammonton, a New England settlement), then hurry onward to the sea, passing by the way the wine-producing settlement of *Egg Harbor City*, and the inland marine village of *Absecon*, famed for its fine oysters. Here the scene changes, and broad green meadows open upon the view, while in the distance, six or seven miles ahead, Atlantic City is plainly seen, with its towers and spires, its cupolas and lighthouse. A new life is awakened on the train; the city, which is not again lost to view, is the subject of attention. Now the bridge which spans the "thoroughfare" is crossed; and soon the long train glides into one of the fine avenues, where, by an admirable arrangement, tourists are left at the door of any of

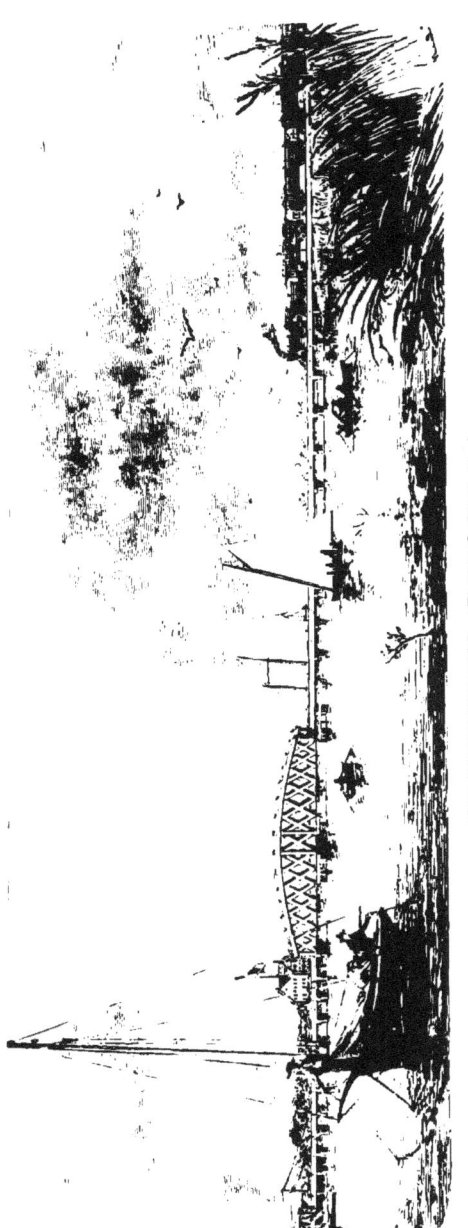

THE THOROUGHFARE, ATLANTIC CITY, N. J.

the principal hotels. A gay scene welcomes the arrival. The piazzas, verandas, and lawns of hotels, boarding-houses, and cottages, are filled with summer visitors, each anxious to discover some coming friend; while carriages dash to and fro, bands of music fill the air with melody, and the scene presents a happy combination of life, animation, and happiness.

The observant visitor needs but a glance to convince him that he has reached a prosperous and well-ordered community. He sees broad, level, and well-graded avenues, stretching away on either side, bordered by shaded walks, and lined with buildings of every variety, from the trim cottage to the extensive summer hotel. Horse-cars, street-lamps, uniformed police, all help to assure him, by their presence, that *Atlantic City* is a city indeed. The success which has followed the establishment of this mammoth summer-resort is remarkable. Twenty years has made it attractive and famous. Its hundred or more hotels and boarding-houses furnish accommodations for forty thousand visitors; and, although the number of houses is constantly increasing, they are taxed to their utmost capacity. Cottages, combining elegance and comfort, adorned by shade-trees and flowers, are springing up with great rapidity.

The location of Atlantic City presents unrivalled facilities for aquatic sports. *Absecon Inlet* is on the north, and *Great Egg Harbor* is on the south; quiet bays cover the rear, while grand old ocean rolls in front. Absecon Inlet is a favorite resort, and of convenient access. It is reached by a pleasant walk along the beach, or, for such as prefer, by the horse-cars, which traverse the city from end to end. Sailing and fishing are the attractive amusements, for which every facility is afforded; numerous fishing-boats, with tackle complete, will be found ready to take parties immediately to the fishing-grounds; and white-winged yachts, in charge of experienced boatmen, to sail on the quiet bays, or start for a dash through old ocean's briny spray. Many others seek entertain-

LANDING-PLACE ON THE INLET.

ment in driving, and, in fashionable equipages, dash across the hardened beach, which for ten miles extends along the coast.

Two miles of fine plank walk have been constructed for the use of guests, where crowds of visitors promenade, or, seated in the many pavilions which dot the scene, watch the sportive games of the bathers, thousands of whom daily enjoy that exhilarating sport.

For those who prefer indoor bathing, Atlantic City has facilities possessed by no other seaside resort, namely, *hot sea-water baths*. Even in the heart of the city an establishment has been erected, with fifty-three of these bath-rooms, arranged for hot and cold water, drawn direct from the ocean. These baths have attracted the especial attention of the medical profession. Dr. Keating, an eminent physician of Philadelphia, thus writes of their advantages : —

"Already have the wants of a class of invalids been provided for in the erection of a large and commodious bathing-establishment, on a scale

EXCURSION HOUSE, ATLANTIC CITY, N.J.

unequalled in this country, where the paralyzed, the weak and timid, can all enjoy the inestimable benefits arising from hot and cold salt-baths and shower-baths. Medical men alone can estimate the value of such an enterprise; and it is not difficult to predict the result to a class of invalids who have hitherto been precluded, by their very condition, from deriving much benefit from a sea-side residence."

The air of Atlantic City has a dryness peculiar and remarkable, and is highly recommended for its healthfulness by the physicians of Philadelphia. On this subject Dr. Keating writes as follows: —

"Some fifteen years since I visited Atlantic City; and, with many others,* I was struck with the peculiarity of its position, the distinctive characteristics of its climate, the singular dryness of its atmosphere, rendering it in many respects one of the most lovely, salubrious climates I have ever visited. . . . .

* Among the many eminent medical men who have indorsed my views, I am proud to name the late Professor Jackson, of the University of Pennsylvania, whose far-see-

YACHTING UP THE INLET.

ATLANTIC CITY, N.J.

Bedford Springs.—"No place of summer resort in America enjoys a higher reputation for health-restoring properties than these springs, which are situated in Bedford County, Pennsylvania, one mile south of the town of Bedford. Their waters are classified as *purgative-chalybeate*, and in their properties resemble the springs of Franzensbad, in Bohemia, and several other celebrated *spas* of Europe, where the *mineral mud-bath* is used with great advantage in cases of paralysis, rheumatism, and gout. . . . The waters are recommended for a wide range of diseases, including those of the liver, the kidneys, and the skin, and for some of these ailments are pronounced absolute specifics. . . .

"The springs were discovered in 1804, and the following year were frequented by persons afflicted with diseases, who encamped in the valley to be near the newly-discovered fountain of health. Not long afterward accommodations were provided for visitors; and for three-score years they have regularly drawn a large number of health and pleasure seekers. The natural beauty of the valley where the springs burst forth is great; and it seems to have been formed by nature as a retreat for wearied and suffering humanity. High hills surround it, ascended by terraced walks; and from their summits pleasing vistas open. From the elevated position of these springs among the ranges of the Alleghany Mountains, and the dense forest growth surrounding them, the atmosphere is always deliciously cool; and doubtless much of the benefit derived by visitors is owing to the fact that no suffering is experienced from the midsummer sun, and that refreshing sleep can always be enjoyed."

Bellows Falls, Vt. Bellows Falls, or, as might more properly be said, cataract, forms an object worthy the attention of the sight-seer. It consists of a channel fifty feet in width, cut far down into the solid rock, through which the waters of the Connecticut rivers rush. A descent of fifty feet is made during the passage over which the river tumbles and foams. The scenery in the vicinity is fine, both in richness and variety. Bellows Falls may be reached by any of the railroad lines which strike the Connecticut River above or below.

Prout's Neck, or **Libbey's Neck, Me.**, is a capital place for the tribe who have nautical tastes, and love the pleasures found by "the shores of the sounding sea."

Old Orchard Beach, on the margin of Saco, is as inviting perhaps as any place named in this work, and, when its accommodations are as good, may acquire as great popularity. It is just rural enough, city enough, and homelike when one is fairly settled down, to make a most delicious source of daily pleasure. It is reached by the "Boston and Maine Railroad." (See cut in that article.)

Portland, Me., although not a city for summer rest, but one from which the people pilgrimate in the sweltering months, is far from deficient in local beauties and sights. The traveller who concludes to " do " Portland will find rich materials for his sketch-book and his notations. In fact, if it were not a large city it would be a thronged home of the pleasure-seekers. Its being on the line of travel to the British Provinces gives it great advantages as a halting-place, from which to read up the various attractions offered, and the routes leading to them. This important centre for departure is reached by the " Eastern " and by the " Boston and Maine " Roads from Boston, the " Portland and Ogdensburg," the " Portland and Rochester," and is the Atlantic terminus of the " Grand Trunk."

Cushing's Island, in Portland Harbor, is a charming resort, and should have a day or two of visit if possible. It is a drowsy, dreamy sort of place, and good for those who have been over-eager and hurried with excitements. It is a sure sedative for disturbed nerves.

The Genesee Falls, N.Y., at Rochester, is one of those wild and romantic assemblages of water battles with rocky obstructions, which are ever novel and of exciting interest, — wonderfully enhanced, in the Genesee, from the skilful mastery of its turbulence, by the hand of art and scientific devices.

Sharon Springs, N.Y., have a high name for their health-restoring waters. Reached by stage from New York Central Railroad at Palatine Bridge.

A visit to **Taghkanic Falls, N.Y.**, will find a magnificent plunge, of more than two hundred feet, by a wildly tossing column of water, in vast volume, and rivalling even Niagara itself in some of its grander features. It is an object of much interest to naturalists. By boat from Cayuga, N.Y.

Portsmouth, N.H., has proved an admirable place from which to emigrate. It has one of the best harbors, rears the smartest of men and most charming of women ; but the city persists in not growing in population. It is a grand centre or starting-point, however, from which to visit a vast number of famed and delightful spots ; and it wears a thronged and busy air during the hot months. It is convenient, also, as a " roost " for travelling birds. Go by the " Eastern Railroad."

Frost's Point, near Portsmouth, N.H., is a very pleasant place, and has a local popularity.

WESTERN TRAVEL.

GIBBON the historian dwells glowingly on the highway from end to end of the Roman world; that is, from Glasgow to Jerusalem, a distance of 3,709 miles. But this stupendous work was only one-twelfth the length of the present railroad system of the United States, and was not much longer than the miles of track already laid down in Iowa.

Railroads were in the outset far less perfect, while more complicated and costly, than they have since become. The law of progress has governed them, as it indeed governs every thing. Some Western roads have profited by Eastern experience, and from their beginning have introduced those modern appliances for reducing the *risks of travel to a minimum*, and the *comfort to a maximum*.

Specimens of such improvements are the Miller Platform and Coupler, Westinghouse Safety Air Brake (which would have prevented many of the fearful railway catastrophes which sicken the heart), the Pullman Sleeping and Dining-room Cars, and Passenger Coaches, running through from cities widely distant. Travellers from Europe and the far East wonder at seeing these things beyond the banks of the Mississippi.

The **Chicago, Burlington, and Quincy Railroad**, which extends from Chicago to several terminal points on the Missouri River, is a good illustration of a complete highway. This road crosses the Mississippi at Burlington, on one of the finest iron bridges in the world.

No expense has been spared in its construction. Its length is 2,237 feet, resting on piers of solid masonry 18x155 feet at the bottom, and 9x23 at the top, and rising twelve feet above the highest water-mark known. From Burlington the road extends westward to Leavenworth, Atchison, Kansas City, St. Joseph, Plattsmouth, Nebraska City, and Omaha: at the latter point making direct and close connection with the "Union Pacific" for San Francisco and the Territories. The Hotel Car, most convenient of all modern inducements to travellers, is constantly in use on this line; also the celebrated Pullman Sleeping-Car, wherein the traveller can sleep as comfortably while travelling at the rate of thirty miles an hour as in his own bed at home. It is these adjuncts of travel that make this the favorite route across the continent, a trip which should be taken by all who desire to know more of the customs and scenery of the great and growing West.

Assuming that the traveller is familiar with the route as far as Chicago, or at least that he knows how to get there, let him on any fine morning take the 10.15 train on the Chicago, Burlington, and Quincy Railroad, *than which there is no better in the country, en route* for San Francisco. For the first few miles he will be surprised and delighted with the large number of suburban towns, and the completeness of their construction and adornment. Some rival the suburbs of our Eastern cities.

The "Illinois Central Railroad" crosses our route at Mendota, which place we reach after three hours' ride. Here dinner awaits us, the quality and abundance of which are among the noticeable features; and, what is better than all, we have a plenty of time in which to discuss it. Again we are *en route*; and the train is whirled along an immense prairie region, through fields of corn, studded with enterprising towns and thriving farms. At 6. P.M., we reach Galesburg; yet so evenly ballasted is this road that we have not yet thought of fatigue. Galesburg seems like a New England town, magically transplanted to a Western State. The society also is said to be unexceptionable; and few places East or West exhibit more taste or refinement.

PLEASANT VALLEY,
Pacific R.R.

Here a Hotel Car is attached to the train. The safety, pleasure, and comforts of railroad travel have been wonderfully improved during the last few years, but this, one of the latest, will unquestionably be pronounced the *best* of the comfort-seeking inventions yet produced. For the extremely low sum of seventy-five cents the wants of "the inner man" are supplied, — broiled steak and quail, and cakes smoking hot, and no cry of "All aboard!" from the conductor. In a word, while moving without exertion through the air like a bird of passage, we eat, drink and sleep, surrounded by the luxuriant ease and comforts of home; and passengers thus sumptuously regaled are lost to distance. With the setting sun we find ourselves approaching the Mississippi, "the Father of Rivers." It is here spanned by another of those splendid iron bridges, across which we glide to the city of Burlington. With what a feeling of confidence we cross the mighty stream! Not a jar mars the pleasure of the passage. Burlington is one of the most enterprising and thriving cities of the West; and its location is unexceptional. With the closing darkness we leave the city behind; and, as the curtains of night shut out the rich landscape, we draw our own curtains about us, and resign ourselves to a night of rest, and with our closing thoughts ask blessings for the man that invented the Pullman Sleeping-Car. The morning finds us at Council Bluffs, on the east bank of the Missouri, five hundred miles west from Chicago. We have crossed the fertile State of Iowa. At 11. A.M., we pass the river, still borne by a magnificent iron bridge, to Omaha. Here we strike the line of the "Union Pacific Railroad;" and four days hence, transported through scenes unequalled on the continent, without leaving the car, we are safely landed on the Pacific coast.

Mount Desert, Me., is the rising star of Maine's attractions for the summer-home seekers. Apart from any little side-shows which may have been put up in the papers from time to time by shrewd and calculating capitalists, Mount Desert has gifts that are all its own, and such as will continue to swell its fame as years progress, and its charms become revealed. Its area is reckoned at about a hundred square miles; and it is, therefore, quite a little world in itself. The island might aptly be likened to a lot of marbles dropped from the pocket of a giant, provided a giant's marbles were small mountains. At least, the more notable and striking portions of the island are made up of a group of mountains huddled together, and of a singularly wild grandeur. Upon one portion there is a sheer and almost vertical descent of rock, nearly a thousand feet from the brink to the deep water below; and the progress of the explorer is constantly met by changes and surprises of panoramic and kaleidoscopic beauty. Much fine soil is found, and is considerably cultivated; but the inhabitants are chiefly absorbed in fish-catching. Portions of Mount Desert are still primeval in their solitudes; and Nature yet prevails in her simplicity and peculiar sovereignty. Hence wild game may still be hunted; and sylvan streams are enriched by great numbers of the gamey trout. The indications within a few years are unmistakable that Mount Desert will take a rank among the families of the wealthy and fashionable second to none on the coast, or even the continent. As soon as the needed capital determines to invest, and the newspapers open their trumpet throats to proclaim Mount Desert and "all about it," the armies of summer pilgrims will commence the mighty march to grand and glorious Mount Desert. "Boston and Maine" or "Eastern Railroad" to Portland, and thence by steamers of the Portland, Bangor, and Machias Steamboat Company.

Lynn, Mass., is a busy and thriving city, famed as the leading shoe-manufacturing place on the continent. A lofty and commanding eminence called High Rock, from which a singularly picturesque view is obtained, is the chief point of attraction to the traveller. The "Eastern Railroad" and horse-cars from Boston pass through the city.

Swampscott, adjoining Lynn, is a favorite with the wealthy classes of Boston and neighboring cities, and has numerous costly and elaborate summer residences. The chief industry of the place is fishing; and a very clever addition to the season's profits is made by letting rooms and dwellings during the summer months. It is accessible by the "Eastern Railroad," and horse-cars from Boston.

Deer Isle, just at Penobscot Bay, is notably famous for its healthful atmosphere, of which some remarkable stories are told. Deer Isle has won considerable reputation among a certain class, who are satisfied with plain living, wholesome food, good, pure air, and freedom from formal restraints. Reached from Portland, Me.

Seneca Falls, N.Y., which are the outlet of Seneca Lake, may be studied *en route* to a sojourn at the charming lake. The whole region is replete with novelties and striking objects. It is said that the lake never freezes over. However this may be in winter, it is certain that its playful charms are all open and unsealed in summer. By steam-cars from Cayuga, N.Y. See description "Northern Central R.R."

Suspension Bridge, which is regarded as one of the world's wonders, and safely spans the fierce currents of Niagara, will not be omitted by any traveller whose course lies in that famed region. It is eight hundred feet long, and about two hundred and sixty feet above the flood. The New York Central, Erie, and Great Western trains cross this structure.

Casco Bay, Me., the musical waters whereof sing sweet songs, even up to the margin of the discordant city, — Casco Bay seems expressly formed for the lovers of the romantic, the beautiful, and the wonderful. Here Nature has nestled the charms of the sea and of the land in almost every variety, — in miniature continents, rivers, hills, valleys, bluffs, beaches, wild rocks, soft verdure, fragrant flowers, and birds of richest plumage and sweetest song. Indeed, the dullest nature is moved with unwonted stirrings, approaching the poetic; and the man of sensibility feels a pleasure rarely found, and all the more keen that the noisy and disorderly crowd have not yet invaded this undefiled paradise of the sea and shore. Whoever cannot find true satisfaction amid the beauties of Casco Bay must be made of the cheapest and poorest mortal clay.

Sharon Springs "should also be visited while making this trip. This favorite resort is in Schoharie County, New York. The village is delightfully located 'in a valley on a hill,' and is surrounded by attractive scenery, through which are lovely drives and promenades. Sulphur, magnesia, and chalybeate springs gush out within a space of a few rods of each other; and their healing virtues have been known for more than half a century,— particularly for their effect in cutaneous disorders. From the village a grand and beautiful prospect opens to the north and east, embracing hills, woods, villages, and streams like silver threads, closely resembling a gorgeous piece of tapestry. Within easy distance is **Tekaharawa Falls**, caused by a small brook precipitating itself over a wall of rock, in a secluded hemlock ravine, a distance of one hundred and fifty feet; and, twenty miles away, by railroad, is **Howe's Cave**, — a wonderful natural curiosity, which has been explored for seven miles."

Wells Beach — we are now in Maine — is a very long, fine, and firm drive-way, which gives considerable popularity to it as a summer resort. But the gunners go there to drive the sea-fowl to remoter and less noisy beaches, free from fine guns and poor shots; and the fishermen to practise their favorite amusement. The "Boston and Maine Railroad" passes near.

Little Boar's Head, North Hampton, N.H., is a connecting link between Hampton and Rye Beaches. It would be famous but for the superiority of its great rival, Boar's Head. It is a projection, also, into the sea, but of a lesser altitude. These marked spots, adjacent to such grand beaches as Hampton and Rye, are assured of a constant popularity. It is a favorite summer resort for families of taste and refinement. The sea-view from the two promontories reaches out far beyond the famous Isles of Shoals. The trip is made by the "Eastern Railroad."

Stonington, R. I. — Although Stonington possesses considerable reputation as a summer resort, it is better known to the travelling public as the New England terminus of the Stonington Line of Sound Steamers, which by their stanch construction and admirable management have won for themselves a position second to none of the numerous fleet of coast-wise boats from New York.

Newburyport, Mass., is an ancient but pleasant city as a residence; but its commercial trade has been absorbed by Boston.

Plum Island, a few miles from Newburyport, possesses a local reputation. It is a favorite place for camping out by the sea; but it is, in the main, a great sand farm.

Route from Washington and the South, through Baltimore, Harrisburg, Williamsport, and Elmira, to Watkins Glen and Niagara Falls.

WASHINGTON, D.C., FROM ARLINGTON HEIGHTS.

A BIRD'S-EYE view of the metropolis of the nation, from a spot associated with so many historic memories, can scarcely fail to interest the tourist. Beneath the central dome of the picture are supposed to congregate the assembled wisdom of the nation, drawn to Washington to deliberate upon the important questions of the day. Here, too, assemble the beauty and gayety of the country, whose encouraging presence gives zest to the debate, and whose cheering hospitality gives relief from the labors of the hour.

THE CAPITOL stands on an eminence ninety feet above tide-water. The site was selected by George Washington; and the corner-stone was laid by him Sept. 18, 1793. It was first occupied by Congress on the third Monday of November, 1800. On the 24th of August, 1814, the interior was destroyed by fire by British troops. In 1850 Congress voted an extension, the corner-stone of which was laid by President Fillmore, July 4, 1851. The statue of America, which surmounts the present dome, is two hundred and ninety-six feet and six inches above the ground. The plan of the city embodies two sets of streets, one set running with the four *cardinal points*, across which the avenues run diagonally.

The stranger should also visit the Executive Mansion; State, Treasury, War, Navy, Post-Office, and Interior Departments; Patent Office; Smithsonian Institute, &c.

In times past a visit to Washington from remote sections of the country was an event of no ordinary character. Weeks were consumed in performing what a few hours will now accomplish. Perhaps the most important improvement of recent date is the completion of the **Baltimore and Potomac Railway**, by the **Northern Central**, and its great ally the **Pennsylvania Railroad**, from *Baltimore* through *Washington* to *Quantico*, Va., a point of junction with the "Richmond, Fredericksburg, and Potomac" Railroad, securing an unbroken railway connection with the South Atlantic and Gulf States, the North, and the Great West.

ENTRANCE TO BALTIMORE TUNNEL.

This line connects with the Northern Central, by tunnel through Baltimore, at the northern limit of the city. Here also connection is made with the Union Railroad, designed as a connecting link with the Philadelphia, Wilmington, and Baltimore Railroad, and through it with the railroad system of the Middle and New-England States, by which trains now pass through Baltimore without the aid of horses.

The **Northern Central Railroad**, which commences at Baltimore, and runs almost due north through Maryland and Pennsylvania, penetrating into the State of New York as far as Canandaigua, offers to the tourist and traveller a variety of beautiful scenery unsurpassed on the American Continent.

The Excursion.

Leaving Baltimore at 7.30 in the morning, provided with elegant coaches, Westinghouse air-brakes, and all the modern appliances which add to the comfort or safety of the passenger, we move through the northern suburbs of the city, and pass along "Jones Falls," a small stream, seemingly insignificant as it creeps lazily over its rocky bed, but which has caused the city fathers of Baltimore much anxiety as to "what they will do with it." Seven miles from Baltimore we break suddenly upon "Lake Roland," a small but beautiful sheet of water, the source from which a populous city draws its supply. For twenty miles we pass through a rich limestone valley, where the abundant crops give token of the richness of the soil. The road follows the tortuous course of the stream, affording at every turn new and pleasing views. Thirty-five miles from Baltimore we cross the Maryland line, and enter Pennsylvania. Passing through a rich agricultural district, filled with substantial farm-houses and small villages we arrive at Hanover Junction. At this point connection is made with the railroad to Gettysburg, thirty miles distant, where that memorable battle was fought that obtained for it the name of the "Waterloo of America," and which will make it a place of interest for all time.

FROM THE TIDE WATERS OF THE SOUTH TO THE PICTURESQUE REGIONS OF THE NORTH.

Soon after leaving Hanover Junction the spires of the borough of York are seen in the distance. We are whirled rapidly along, now and again catching glimpses of the substantially built portion of the town. York is a thriving borough of some twelve thousand inhabitants, the county-seat of York County, and the centre of a rich farming district.

During the invasion of Pennsylvania in June, 1863, it was laid under contribution by Gen. Early. Twelve bridges on the line of the Northern Central Road were burned at the same time, and nineteen on the "Wrightsville Branch," which extends from York to Wrightsville, and thence by the "Columbia Branch" to Lancaster, where connection is made with the Pennsylvania Railroad.

After a stop at York of five minutes we are away again; and ere long we reach the banks of the beautiful Susquehanna. On we speed, the noble river on our right flowing calmly onward to the sea. We are now approaching Harrisburg, the capital of Pennsylvania. The river, as we glide along its banks, with its attractive scenery, its islands and rocks, with the town beyond, affords a view of unusual beauty.

THE SUSQUEHANNA.

The numerous islands and huge masses of rock with which the broad bosom of the river is studded lend the charm of variety to the scenery. Now and again long bridges span the noble stream; villages are seen on the opposite shore; and for fifty miles we have a changing panorama of river scenery.

Harrisburg is reached by the Northern Central, over a bridge a mile in length; the trains running on the top. Nothing obstructs the prospect up or down the river; and the slow rate of speed allows a good five minutes' view of rare loveliness from a car window. Harrisburg is the point of connection with the "Pennsylvania," the "Cumberland Valley," and the "Philadelphia and Reading" Railroads. Here a magnificent Pullman Parlor Car is added to our train, and a coach from Philadelphia. These are run daily between Philadelphia, and Watkins and Rochester, N.Y.

HARRISBURG, PA.
Northern Central Railroad.

The city of *Harrisburg* is pleasantly located, overlooking the Susquehanna, which is here spanned by two fine bridges a mile in length, connecting Harrisburg with *Bridgeport*, from which point the above view was sketched.

Having made connection with the train from Philadelphia, we again continue our course up the banks of the Susquehanna. The scenery is one unbroken panorama of loveliness, — a combination of views, either of which would make the reputation of any popular resort. Approaching *Sunbury*, the conductor calls out, "Passengers for Shamokin, Mt. Carmel, &c., change cars." This is the terminus of the main line of the Northern Central Railway, one hundred and thirty-eight miles from Baltimore; and here connection is made with the "Philadelphia and the Erie" Railroad, extending in a northwesterly direction through Pennsylvania to *Erie*, a distance of two hundred and eighty-eight miles. This road, forty miles of which unite the main line of the Northern Central with its leased roads north of Williamsport, is leased and operated by the Pennsylvania Railroad. From Sunbury we pass up the valley of the West Branch of the Susquehanna to Williamsport. A sumptuous dinner awaits us at the "Herdic House," which is one of the best hotels in Pennsylvania. Fifty-two miles above we reach *Renova Springs*, a resort of great beauty and growing popularity.

RENOVA HOUSE.

At *Williamsport* the "Northern Central" road leaves the Susquehanna, continuing northward up *Lycoming Creek*, which it crosses nineteen times in twenty-six miles. High hills broken into a thousand forms hem it in, many rising into mountain-peaks which cut sharply against the sky. Waterfalls spring from their rugged sides, and are lost in the tangled growth below. The valley is narrow, in places a mere cañon, yet rich in the washings of ages. *Ralston* is the first place of note on this division.

The cool and invigorating atmosphere, the grand scenery, excellent trout-fishing, and good fare have already secured for this locality an unusually large number of guests during the summer months.

This is a good illustration of the scenery in the vicinity. This stream is famous for the number, variety, and beauty of its waterfalls. The whole region possesses great attractions for the artist and lover of nature. It is also noted for the number of its trout brooks and abundance of fish, affording an excellent opportunity for the follower of Izaak Walton to beguile the lonely hours far away from the haunts of men; also an abundance of deer and other game in their season. Is it strange, then, that this picturesque region is rapidly growing in favor with tourists and pleasure-seekers?

Four miles above Ralston we reach *Roaring Creek*, a name significant of the wild scenery of the neighborhood. A good hotel furnishes accommodations for visitors. A more productive soil covers the hills; many are cultivated far up their slopes. Occasionally wild torrents are seen hurrying down the mountain sides, at places forming beautiful cascades. We are nearing the summit; the country opens; and broader fields meet the eye. The water with the descending grade now turns northward; and the train flies rapidly on. The village of *Canton* is next reached. We have now fairly left the mountains; broad cultivated fields stretch far up the neighboring hills, which with gentle undulations surround the town. A picturesque stream finds its way through the valley opening to the east.

Minnequa Springs, a popular summer resort, is only two miles beyond.

DUTCHMAN'S RUN RALSTON PA.

Minnequa is chiefly noted for the medicinal character of its waters. *Alba*, the next station, is a quiet hamlet nestled among the hills. From this place to *Troy* the scenery possesses little to interest the traveller; but *Troy* is a delightful village, handsomely located, and contains many beautiful private residences and several churches. *Sugar Creek* flows through the village, which adds to the picturesque beauty of the place.

From Troy to *Elmira* the railroad runs through an agricultural country with valleys flanked by high hills. These become less abrupt as they meet those bounding the valley of the *Chemung*, which, crossing at right angles, extends nearly fifty miles east and west, between the *Susquehanna River* and *Painted Post*: *Elmira* being about midway, the largest and most thrifty city in Southern New York. It has a population of twenty thousand. The city is built on an extended plain, bounded by chains of lofty hills, some of which admit of cultivation to their very summits, while others are crowned by heavy woodland. The streets are broad, crossing each other at right angles, and are lined with shade-trees. The *Chemung River* flows through the midst of the city, and is spanned by three iron bridges, one of which is completed. Elmira, the seat of several very prosperous manufacturing interests, is also surrounded by a rich agricultural region, and is the great railway centre of Southern New York. The "Erie" running east and west, and the "Lehigh Valley" and "Northern Central" from the south, unite here, and continue north and westward, connecting with the "Great Western." The "Utica, Ithaca, and Elmira" Railway will also have its terminus here. Many features of mechanical industry will interest the tourist. The Elmira Rolling Mills are the most important in the State, and turn out daily large quantities of railroad rails and merchantable iron. The La France Rotary Pump and Steam Engine Manufactory is attracting great attention among practical men, and will repay an examination from those interested. The Pullman Car, which contributes to the comfort and enjoyment of so many, is built here; also the Erie Car Shops, and many wholesale boot and shoe manufactories, all testifying to the growing importance of this manufacturing centre.

Elmira is also an immense coal-distributing point, for both anthracite and bituminous from the "Lehigh Valley" and the "Northern Central" Railroads. The Pittston and Elmira Coal Company, and Langdon & Co., with principal offices in this city, handle over half a million tons of anthracite annually; while the MacIntyre Coal Company mine and ship through this city three hundred thousand tons annually of bituminous coal from Ralston, Penn., fifty miles south.

Elmira's educational institutions are celebrated. The Female College has a national reputation; and its buildings and grounds are an ornament to the city.

Young ladies from all sections of the country secure here that practical and finished education which fits them for the highest positions in life.

The scenery in the suburbs, along the valleys, and over the hills, is delightful; and through the munificence of one of her citizens, Dr. Edwin Eldridge, Elmira has one of the finest public parks in the country. One hundred and sixty acres of land, wild and uncultivated, in the western suburbs of the city, have been changed into a place of beauty and resort. A charming lake adorns the centre; fountains of exquisite design send up their cooling spray; graded drives and walks are laid out through the grounds, which are ornamented by beautiful statuary and rare exotics, — all for the use of the public, " without money and without price." Should the visitor chance to remain at Elmira over Sunday, he can here witness a novel sight. Among the many attractions of Eldridge Park, a pagoda shaped stand has been erected, surrounded by rustic seats, with capacity for thousands. The grateful shade of a deep green grove is the protection.

HATHEWAY HOUSE.

Numberless birds sing their love-songs in the branches, which, with the soft murmur of the miniature waves chafing on the gravelly beach, fill with music the balmy atmosphere already redolent with the perfumes of rare flowers. Here on each sabbath afternoon (through the thoughtfulness of the donor) a full band discourses soft and melodious music; and at 4 o'clock the Rev. Thomas K. Beecher addresses the assembled multitude.

The great thoroughfares of travel leading from *New England*, *New York*, *Philadelphia*, *Baltimore*, and the *South* concentrate at Elmira. The **Hatheway House**, the favorite stopping-place, has to the travelling public a fine reputation for the excellence of its accommodations and its *cuisine*, and is excelled by few hotels in the country. Resting under this hospitable roof, the tourist has his option to proceed in any direction on the resumption of his journey. The scenery to *Watkins, N. Y.*, is still fine.

We are rapidly approaching a section of country noted for its deep gorges, or glens, cut far down the solid rock by the action of running streams. These form a great variety of water views, of which the accompanying cut of **Empire Fall**, *Glen Excelsior*, is a fine illustration. These falls are on the east side of the valley, near the head of Seneca Lake, not in sight from the road, but are visited from Watkins in a small steamer which plies on the lake for the accommodation of excursion parties.

EMPIRE FALL — GLEN EXCELSIOR.

Empire Fall consists of a series of cascades, falling 106 feet to the valley below. *Havana* is the most important village passed between Elmira and Watkins, and is but four miles from the latter place. It is a quiet, pleasant village, and is remarkable for its glens, waterfalls, and cascades. The falls leap from a great height almost into the streets of the village. There is also a mineral spring at Havana. The intricacies of its glens contain many interesting features; and, whenever the hotels are improved, this must become a place of great resort.

We are moving directly north. The narrow valley from which we have debouched has opened to a mile in width, and is so level that one can but think that the lake, near at hand, at some time covered it. The ground rises on either side precipitously, beyond which evidently lies a table-land drained by streams, which, finding their way to the brink, rush impetuously down the mountain steep, producing a succession of cascades, waterfalls, and pools, connected by deep cavernous gorges. These cañons, or glens, have been known since the settlement of this part of the country, but existed as a matter of course, exciting little interest or attention from the inhabitants of the region. Indeed, from their nature they were very little visited, it being impossible to fully explore them, except by a slow and expensive system of engineering. The most important, best fitted up, and extensively known, of these is **Watkins Glen**. The stream which forms it comes down the mountain from the west, reaching the valley near the head of *Seneca Lake*, where a village of some 3000 inhabitants has sprung up. A horse-railroad continuing up the main street, passes the entrance to the Glen; for those who prefer to walk, the distance is short. On leaving the cars, the tourist is beset by the runners and porters of a half-dozen hotels, making it advisable for him to decide beforehand where he will bestow his patronage, or where he can be best accommodated. As most persons visit Watkins to see the "Glen," it is not surprising that the **Glen Mountain House** should be the popular hotel, although we would not infer that excellent accommodations will not be furnished at several of the others. The proprietors of the Glen Mountain House

GLEN MOUNTAIN HOUSE,
Watkins Glen, N.Y.

are also the owners of the Glen. It is through their enterprise, at the expense of many thousand dollars, that the difficulties of entering and following this curious place have been overcome. Bridges have been constructed, stairways erected, pathways cut in the solid rock, allowing the hidden intricacies and picturesque beauties of this great natural curiosity to be traced, even by ladies or children, for full three miles. It is a weird spot,—not a direct cañon, but more properly a succession of *glens*, or gorges, rising one above another, which form a series of galleries and grottoes, with frequent waterfalls and cascades, often widening out into vast amphitheatres, the grandeur and magnificence of which is indescribable. Its course is nearly east and west; and the total fall of the stream through its tortuous windings is nearly a thousand feet. In places it is quiet and limpid, moving lazily along, reflecting truthfully the trees and rocks which hem it in, and the rich foliage with which it is hung. Suddenly it leaps from a dizzy height, falling a broken, boiling mass, down some deep abyss, then hurries on in endless whirl to repeat the scene. The depth of this gorge varies from **75 to 300 feet.** In places the sides recede, and are covered with foliage.

EAST VIEW OF THE ORIGINAL GLEN MOUNTAIN HOUSE.

Again the rugged steep falls sheer down hundreds of feet, overhanging in places till the branches of the trees which crown its summit interlace.

About a half mile from the entrance of the Glen, perched upon and overhanging the cliff, with the boiling stream far below, stands the **Glen Mountain House**. Deep hemlocks and other evergreens wrap it in perpetual shade. It consists of two buildings, standing on opposite sides of the Glen, connected by a light iron bridge, with a covered way for pedestrians. The original Mountain House was a Swiss structure, unique in design, and tasteful in construction; indeed, it is so artistically adapted to the scenery that it seems a part of it. Its verandas and stairways, galleries and corridors, furnish abundant sources of comfort to guests. But with the increasing popularity of this resort additional accommodations were required;

GLEN MOUNTAIN HOUSE.
(Looking up.)

and the new house was erected on the opposite side. This building is divided into suites and single rooms, while the "Cottage" contains the dining-room and culinary apartments. The Glen Mountain House has been pleasantly located and arranged to secure to guests the maximum amount of comfort. Situated in the midst of this wonderful scenery, it is convenient at all times to run out or in and study its singular characteristics. As few persons are satisfied with one passage through the Glen, the guests of this house find its proximity to the places they would visit of great advantage. Continuing above the house, these beauties are constantly repeating themselves, and, if possible, increasing in grandeur. From the entrance up, each successive scene has received an appropriate name.

Engraved expressly for "Bachelder's Popular Resorts, and How to Reach Them."
RAINBOW FALLS, WATKINS GLEN, N.Y.

Rainbow Falls is, perhaps, one of the most interesting features of the Glen. With the bright sheen of a summer's day playing in the rising mists, the scene is frequently clothed in rainbow tints, but nowhere with such brilliant hues or perfect arch as at *Rainbow Falls;* and the hour of four on every afternoon finds a crowd of guests worshipping at its shrine.

Above the house, the Glen extends for miles, embodying many remarkable features. The " Cathedral " is the most imposing. This is an immense amphitheatre, with walls of solid rock rising to the perpendicular height of three hundred feet, while the forest trees with which the top is fringed stretch their arms far over the yawning gulf. Into this mighty chasm the waters spring with a frightful leap, bathing its sides with feathery spray, then quietly spreading over the rocky floor. The atmosphere, even in the hottest day, is cool and moist. Trees of primeval growth, hardy shrubs, and luxuriant vines cling with wild forms of beauty from the interstices of the rock, reflecting their rich foliage in the emerald pools beneath, while far above is seen the bright blue sky; and at times the rich sunlight, reflecting from cliff to cliff, clothes all with a soft, mellow glow.

HECTOR FALLS, SENECA LAKE, N.Y.

The interest in this region is by no means exhausted with a visit to Watkins Glen. *Havana Glen,* already alluded to, is reached by coaches from the Glen Mountain House. It possesses many curious and interesting features, and will well repay a visit. *Hector Falls* is also a point of interest, and should be included in the visit to Empire Falls.

These are situated on the east side of Seneca Lake, but a few miles distant, and are reached by a small steamer. Neither should the sojourner at Watkins Glen miss a sail on Seneca Lake, one of the most beautiful bodies of water in the world, varying from one-half to six miles in width, and forty miles long. It is of remarkable depth and purity, and in the coldest weather never freezes over.

SENECA LAKE, N.Y.

From Watkins, trains on the "Northern Central" continue along the western shore of Seneca Lake forty-seven miles to Canandaigua, N.Y., where connection is made with the New-York Central Railroad for Albany or Niagara Falls. The route is pleasant, and possesses many points of interest, especially along the shore of the lake, where several waterfalls will be pointed out by the intelligent conductors, if requested. By an admirable arrangement, the cars run through from Baltimore to Rochester. From Rochester to Niagara Falls the country is level, and has few attractions for the traveller. Soon we hear the "roar of Niagara;" and, if our journey is uninterrupted, in sixteen hours after leaving Baltimore, we may be domiciled at some of the mammoth hotels for which the place is celebrated.

The Isles of Shoals, off Portsmouth Harbor, have risen to wonderful fame within twenty years. Fifty years ago it was one of the places to visit, and have a chowder, and was noted for its wild and rugged features even in those prosaic days. It is now a fixture in popular favor, and is visited by multitudes, who make a marked stay there in summer time. Its chief interest lies in its remoteness from the land, and its home in the sea. The entire scene is wild, grim, and barren, excepting the homelike comforts which enterprise and money have supplied.

We have written of "The Isles of Shoals" as "it," although there are half a dozen islands in the group; but we have always associated the places with the idea of but one. And old people still call them "Isle of Shoals;" and this is not far from correct. The eccentric Leighton, who really laid the foundation for the present great fame of this resort of pleasure, faithfully believed that no person coming there, however sick, could die of disease if the invalid remained. Mr. Leighton, although living to a good old age, now rests with his fathers.

Narraganset Pier, R.I. — This is a summer resort of considerable popularity. It is reached by steamboats from Newport and Providence, and by stage from the *Kingston* Station of the "Providence and Stonington Railway." Its isolation has kept it from assuming the importance which its attractiveness warrants.

Marblehead, Mass., is an old place, and bears many marks of its antiquity. It possesses some very attractive surroundings, but has no notable attractions of its own, although it has a full share of visitors.

Lowell Island, about four miles down the harbor from Salem, Mass., and near Marblehead, is without any other inviting qualities than its isolation. In this respect it is attractive. At times its one large hotel has been filled with busy and gay throngs; but, through its difficulty of access, it has failed to maintain a profitable popularity. Fishing from boats or off the rocks is good. It is reached by the "Eastern Railroad" to Marblehead or Salem, and thence by steam-yacht.

Tinker's Island, near to Marblehead, Mass., is a famous place for sea-perch and tautog fishing, but enjoys only a local popularity.

New London, Conn., although a small and tasteful city, will hardly be classed as a summer resort. It nevertheless secures many visitors and admirers. The "Shore Line Railroad" passes through the place, the cars of which are ferried across the head of the harbor. The location is very sightly, and commands some admirable views. Its fine shade-trees give to its homelike dwellings an air of comfort and cultivated taste.

Ebensburg, "the seat of justice of Cambria County, Penn., is situated on the western slope of the Alleghany Mountains, eleven miles from Cresson, with which point it is connected by a branch railroad. The situation of the town is very near the mountain summit; and from the centre of its main street the horizon sinks away in all directions, — the sun setting below the level of the observer. Dense forests of hemlock, beech, and other varieties of American mountain woods, are accessibl in all directions; and the roads leading through them afford delightful drives, while bringing into view many bits of charming scenery, relieved by the soft ferns and thick-growing laurel, nourished to perfection by the limpid waters everywhere issuing from the gigantic mountain. Its altitude gives Ebensburg a delightfully cool and bracing atmosphere, — the air coming freely from the long reaches of primeval verdure, laden with a rich aroma, as grateful to the senses as it is invigorating to the system. For years the town has been a favorite resort for families, who come here early in the season, and remain until the frosts of autumn indicate a return of salubrity to the crowded cities. The accommodations provided for these sojourners are on an extensive scale; and probably as much quiet enjoyment is to be had here as at any place of the kind in America."

Chelsea, Mass., was one of Starr King's favorite spots for sightseeing. "Powder-horn Hill," with its remarkable pictures extending over a circle of miles, was a special object of frequent visits with the scholarly and enthusiastic young preacher, — the rising or the setting of the sun being his chosen times for studying its wonderful beauties. The name has been arbitrarily altered to "The Highlands," which is more pretentious, certainly; but old names, after all, cling closest to historic associations. A hotel now invites visitors to rest and prolonged enjoyment upon this lofty height. The "Eastern Railroad" and horse-cars from Boston pass through the city.

Chelsea Beach (**Revere, Mass.**) is no part of Chelsea proper: it possesses many points of interest, and its proximity to Boston makes it a place of great resort in the hot months. A line of horse-cars connects it with Boston.

The town of **Hampton, N. H.**, has little to distinguish it from towns of modest pretensions generally; but its beach — Hampton Beach — is renowned in every quarter. *Boar's Head*, a bold and commanding promontory, projecting a quarter of a mile from the mainland directly into the sea, is the hospitable castle which "lords it" over the adjacent beaches. Here the admirer of the murmuring sea can find full scope for his admiration. The views from this lofty eminence are numberless and varied. Reached by the " Eastern Railroad."

BOSTON, CONCORD, AND MONTREAL R. R.

THE increase of travel to the White Mountains during the past few years has been something remarkable. The ease with which the trip can now be made, even by the aged or by invalids, has wrought this change. Cars of the most approved styles, equipped with all modern improvements, are run through without change from Boston and from the New-York boats. Hotels furnished with the comforts and luxuries of home spring up from the depths of the forest, and even crown the rocky summit of Mount Washington. A commendable emulation has actuated the several railroad companies, each striving to excel the other by adding to the comforts and conveniences of tourists.

To-day the **Boston, Concord, and Montreal Railroad** leads the van by placing its patrons at the end of their journey with the least effort to themselves. Its rails stretch to the base of Mount Washington; nay, by the patronage of this road, the cars now climb to the crest of that grand old peak, where they deposit travellers on the platform of an excellent hotel which has been built to shelter them. With the exception of a short ride from the Fabyan House to the Mount Washington R.R. Depot (six miles), there is a continuous line from Boston to the top of Mount Washington. This route receives more patronage, and distributes its patrons through more connecting lines, than any other.

Among the most prominent roads which contribute to swell the travel on the Boston, Concord, and Montreal, are the Portsmouth and Concord Railroad, Boston and Maine, Manchester and Lawrence, and Concord, with passengers from *Boston, Lynn, Salem, Lawrence, Manchester*, and the East; the Boston, Lowell, and Nashua, with guests from those cities; Framingham and Lowell, and its connections, with passengers from *New Bedford, Newport, Taunton, Fall River*, and *Providence*, and the *New-York* and *Stonington* lines of steamers; the Worcester and Nashua, with its local and *New-York* travel; and the Connecticut-River and Passumpsic Railways, with their numerous branches and connecting lines. Each of these roads must send its White-Mountain travel over the rails of the Boston, Concord, and Montreal.

Passengers from *Boston* should take the cars at the Boston and Maine Depot (see page 17) or at the Lowell Depot (see page   ). These trains unite at *Manchester, N.H.*, and continue through *Concord* to the **Fabyan House,** at the base of Mount Washington. This route is made pleasant and interesting by the many streams and bodies of water along which it passes, among which may be mentioned the *Charles* and *Mystic* Rivers; the *Merrimac*, along whose banks it follows for many miles; the *Suncook* and *Winnepesaukee* Rivers; Lake *Winnesquam, Little Bay, Lake Winnepesaukee, Waukawan Lake, Long Pond, Pemigewasset* and

Engraved expressly for Bachelder's "Popular Resorts, and How to Reach Them"

HOOKSETT, N.H.

1. Suncook.
2. Suncook Valley Railroad.
3. Hooksett Falls.
4. Concord Railroad.

Baker's Rivers; the *Connecticut*, *Wells*, *Ammonoosuc*, and *Israel's* Rivers; and many other smaller streams and ponds.

We strike the *Merrimac* at *Lawrence* or *Lowell*, following it past *Manchester* and *Concord*, crossing and re-crossing it at times. The beauty of its course is frequently varied by picturesque falls, affording more improved water-power than any river in the country. The falls at *Lawrence*, *Lowell*, *Amoskeag*, and *Hooksett* are particularly noticeable.

The accompanying cut, representing *Hooksett Falls*, also shows the Suncook Valley Railroad, which leads to *Pittsfield, N.H.*, a thriving and beautiful village nestled among high hills, which are dotted with farm-houses, that are fast becoming popular with boarders from cities.

This route also leads through the heart of the cotton-manufacturing interest of New England; passing *Lawrence*, *Lowell*, and *Manchester*, besides many smaller manufacturing-towns. *Concord*, the beautiful capital city of New Hampshire, possesses many features which make it a favorite resort during the summer and autumn months. It contains about 12,500 inhabitants; yet all are so comfortably domiciled, that it is frequently remarked by strangers "Where do your poor live?" The shaded concrete walks of the city add much to the comfort of visitors.

The State Capitol stands in the centre of a small but beautiful square, handsomely laid out, and ornamented with broad-spreading trees. The structure is of pleasing architecture, built of native granite, for which the vicinity is noted, the whole surmounted by a lofty dome. Immediately fronting the State House, on the main street, is the **Eagle Hotel**, a fine brick structure, which is widely known as a first-class house. The "Eagle" receives much of its foreign patronage from parties, who, after starting for the mountains, prefer to spend a few days at Concord before leaving for the season; and particularly from those returning in the autumn, driven in by the early frosts, who always find here and in the vicinity a few weeks of charming weather.

Among the other public buildings may be named the Court House, Churches, Schools, City Hall, State Prison, and State Asylum for Insane.

The two latter institutions are in fine condition. The Prison, unlike those of many States, is made a paying institution. The Asylum has been built 32 years, and is very successfully conducted.

Concord is somewhat celebrated for its manufactures, particularly of carriages and coaches, which are shipped extensively to all parts of the world. As a railroad centre, Concord presents admirable facilities for intercourse with various sections of the country.

The line proper of the Boston, Concord, and Montreal Railroad starts from Concord, though its cars and those of the Boston, Lowell and Nashua, the Framingham and Lowell, and the Worcester and Nashua Roads, run through from those cities, and continue to the mountains.

Engraved expressly for "Bachelder's Popular Resorts, and How to Reach Them."

TILTON, N.H.

1. Methodist Seminary.
2. Winnepesaukee River.
3. Boston, Montreal, and Concord R.R.
4. Belknap Mountain.

A few miles above Concord, the road again crosses the Merrimac, and leads away towards Lake *Winnepesaukee*.

Tilton is the first town of interest. This was formerly known as *Sanbornton Bridge*. It is a thriving manufacturing village, and forms the centre of a large agricultural region. The Methodist Seminary located here, a good view of which appears in the engraving, has been long and favorably known. *Tilton* possesses an unusually fine water-power, not computed by its volume alone, but by its great regularity. The river which runs through the place is the outlet of *Lake Winnepesaukee*, in which large reservoir the water is held in reserve by the water-power company which owns it, to supply the cotton-manufactories at Lowell and Lawrence during the droughts of summer.

There is a charm in this whole region for summer life. Not only the town of Sanbornton, from which Tilton is an offshoot, but Canterbury and Meredith, Belmont and Gilmanton, all furnish desirable summer homes. The topography is particularly adapted to promote the health of its inhabitants. The land is generally high and rolling, and has been so long cleared that the climate is fully established.

A stage leaves Tilton, on the arrival of the morning train, for **Gilmanton Academy,** passing through *Belmont*, formerly known as Upper Gilmanton. Gilmanton is becoming popular as a summer residence for persons from Boston and New York, who build here houses for the warm season. It possesses the advantage of good and long-established institutions of learning, and is sought by persons having a family. Although supplied with daily mail and stage connections, there is no railroad within its borders; and, with a society cultivated by its fine schools, it possesses much of that pristine character which characterized New England towns of earlier days. *Lower Gilmanton* is reached by the "Concord" and "Suncook Valley Railroad" to Pittsfield, and Gilmanton Iron Works by the "Boston and Maine" to Alton, and thence by stages. From Tilton the road follows the *Winnepesaukee River*, and the shores of *Little Bay* and *Winnesquam Lake*, past *Union Bridge*, to *Laconia*.

Although undeveloped at present, this region possesses many features calculated to make it popular with the seeker after health and pleasure. Winnesquam Lake is some twelve or fifteen miles in length, is beautiful in form and surroundings, and, but for its more pretentious rival Winnepesaukee, would have, ere this, received the attention which its merits deserve. It has long been known as the home for the lake trout, and somewhat famed for its piscatorial advantages. Two small summer houses furnish accommodation for visitors, — the *Winnesquam* at the lower end of the lake, and the *Bay View*, which is admirably located in the suburbs of Laconia. The cars pass between it and the lake, and leave passengers when requested.

Engraved expressly for "Bachelder's Popular Resorts, and How to Reach Them."

LACONIA, N.H.

1. Lake Winnesquam.
2. Sandwich Mountains.
3. Boston, Concord, and Montreal R.R.
4. Bay View House.
5. Mount Belknap.

"This peculiar characteristic is patent to all who have ever sojourned there, and is the distinctive feature of the place, to which I attribute its great advantage over every other sea-bathing resort on the coast. . . . .

"This remarkable dryness of climate resembles more that of Nice on the Mediterranean, than any sea-coast I have ever visited. It is this peculiarity which affords relief and cure to all cases of rheumatic fever and arthritis, even in the most acute stages. I know of many instances in which invalids, after having recourse, without benefit, to the various mineral waters and baths in the country, have, on visiting there, been entirely cured by a summer sojourn. . . . .

"The absence of malaria, and the balminess of the atmosphere, permit a residence at Atlantic City from the middle of May until the middle of November. . . . .

"What an estimable blessing to a city like Philadelphia, with its million of inhabitants, to have, almost as its suburb, within two hours' pleasant ride, a sea-side residence combining such rare hygienic advantages! — to which I would respectfully call the attention of my medical brethren throughout the United States, as it has long been a well-established principle to trust more to hygiene than to actual medication."

Mr. George L. Catlin, in his book on "Sea-Shore Homes," says, —

"But it is to invalid children that this atmosphere of Atlantic City appears to give its most healthful influences; and so well established has this fact become, that a few benevolent Philadelphians have erected here a 'Children's Sea-shore House,' where sick and wasted little ones from the city are furnished support and attendance." The building is large and handsome, with accommodation for fifty or sixty children.

To the pleasure-seeker Atlantic City offers even greater inducements. Bands of music at each prominent hotel daily entertain guests with the choicest selections. "Hops" are of nightly occurrence, attended by the youth and beauty of a dozen cities. Theatricals, concerts, and other entertainments, are regularly given. Elaborate fireworks are frequently exhibited. Few summer resorts offer so many and such varied attractions.

Handsome churches of nearly every denomination are also to be found here. Even the "Friends" have their house of worship.

The top of the Lighthouse is a place of great resort, where thousands go to witness the magnificent panoramic view afforded. Not only the ocean in all its grandeur, but the bays and inlets of this serrated coast, the soft, green meadows, and the wood-clad hills which lie beyond, combine to make this a panoramic view of remarkable variety and beauty.

The tourist, in pursuit of health or pleasure, should not fail to visit Atlantic City.

ing eye and keen judgment caused him, in 1859, to state to me that he considered the atmospheric condition of Atlantic City one of the most peculiar in the country, and that it would in time become available in the treatment of many diseases.

☞ *This page concludes the article on "Atlantic City," and should have followed page 62.*

The route, which from Concord lies through an uninteresting country, now fairly enters the lake and mountain region. The scenery does not possess the grandeur of the White-Mountain section; yet it is marked by many elements of picturesque beauty. Its water-views are fine; a distant line of mountain-peaks cuts the horizon. It is only five miles, over a good country road, to *Mount Belknap*, which is easily accessible, and from whose barren summit may be had one of the finest landscape-views on the Atlantic slope. It varies from the *Red-Hill* prospect by having *Lake Winnepesaukee* and the entire group of the *White* and *Franconia Mountains* in the same view. The steamer "Mount Washington" can be distinctly seen soon after it leaves *Alton Bay*, and traced on its way for more than twenty-five miles to *Wolfboro'* and *Centre Harbor*. The steamer "Lady of the Lake" can also be followed in its tortuous course from *Weir's* to Centre Harbor and Wolfboro'. From this elevated position a much better idea of the great number of islands is obtained than while sailing on the lake. Beyond its placid waters the mountain ranges rise in successive peaks; and towering above all is the well-known "Presidential Group," of which *Mount Washington* is the commanding centre.

Mount Belknap is at present but little known to the travelling public; but its pleasant approach, easy access, and magnificent "View" must eventually bring it into great popularity. Visitors to Laconia will find the **Bay View House** (seen on the right of the engraving) delightfully located, and surrounded by beautiful scenery. It is noted alike for its good table, home-like atmosphere, and reasonable terms.

LAKE VILLAGE, N.H.
Boston, Concord, and Montreal R.R.

Lake Village is but a mile and a half from Laconia; their suburbs meet; and the towns are seemingly one. The views in the vicinity are very like those near Laconia. Indeed, the same mountain ranges may be seen in the distance, though the water foreground is different. There is nothing grand in the scenery as the train steams away towards the lake, but it is very picturesque. At *Weir's Station* passengers change for *Wolfboro'*, *Centre Harbor*, and *Conway*. Within the past year a Methodist camp-meet-

Engraved expressly for "Bachelder's Popular Resorts, and How to Reach Them."

WEIR'S LANDING, N.H.

1. Camp-Meeting Ground.
2. Sandwich Mountains.
3. Boston, Concord, and Montreal R.R.
4. Ossipee Mountains.
5. Lake Winnepesaukee.
6. Steamer "Lady of the Lake."

ing ground has been dedicated in a delightful grove adjoining the station, which bids fair to increase the popularity of this charming spot. Several commodious buildings have already been erected: lots for cottages have been secured on a site commanding a magnificent view of the lake, with fine boat and railroad accommodations. Those who desire to visit *Wolfboro'*, *Centre Harbor*, or *Conway* will find the commodious little steamer **Lady of the Lake** awaiting them at the landing. Arrangements have been made to run the boat from Wolfboro' to Weir's, and *vice versa*, to accommodate tourists to and from the Franconia Mountains. The distance to Wolfboro' is twenty miles, and to Centre Harbor but half that, although the latter route seems to combine all the beauties of the lake. When the steamer leaves the wharf, the jutting points of the adjacent islands would seem to bar our progress; but, as it speeds its way, the view unfolds, the channel opens; and we wind our pleasant course among the islands, at times so near that the overhanging branches almost sweep the boat. The lake is from twenty-five to thirty miles long, and varies from one to eight miles wide. It contains about sixty-nine square miles, and nearly three hundred islands, on many of which are fine farms, and several are used for grazing. Its surface is 472 feet above the level of the sea. The numerous islands which dot its bosom, the beautiful hills which hem it in, and its many points and inlets, combine to make Winnepesaukee one of the most pleasing inland resorts in the country. The sedative influence and peculiar quiet of the scene, during the charming days of an Indian summer, with the bright tints of an autumnal foliage, graduating to the soft haze of the mountain blue, reflected in its waters, is most wonderful. At Centre House or Wolfboro' for days and weeks the tourist lingers, forgetting, among the quiet beauties of nature, the cares of a business-life. The excursion to Centre Harbor also forms one of the most delightful *day-trips* from Boston. Leaving the city at 8 o'clock in the morning, viâ the Boston, Concord, and Montreal R.R. and steamer "Lady of the Lake," the visitor will have an hour for dinner at Centre Harbor, returning by the steamer "Mount Washington," and Boston and Maine Railroad, to Boston the same evening, thus passing through the cities of Lowell, Nashua, Manchester, Concord, Dover, Haverhill, and Lawrence, with the intervening towns, and traversing the entire length and breadth of Lake Winnepesaukee, by both routes, in a single day.

It would be easy to introduce pages of description from the pens of visitors; but all are embodied in the following quotation from that eminent writer, EDWARD EVERETT.

"I have been something of a traveller in our own country, — though far less than I could wish, — and in Europe have seen all that is most attractive,

Engraved expressly for "Bachelder's Popular Resorts, and How to Reach Them."

STEAMER "LADY OF THE LAKE."

Connecting Wier's Landing, Boston Concord, & Montreal R.R., with Wolfboro' and Centre Harbor, N.H.

from the Highlands of Scotland to the Golden Horn of Constantinople, from the summit of Hartz Mountains to the Fountain of Vaucluse; but my eye has yet to rest on a lovelier scene than that which smiles around you as you sail from Weir's Landing to Centre Harbor."

From *Weir's Landing* the train continues northward past *Meredith*, a pleasant village located on the shores of the lake, from which steamers run to other villages during portions of the year. Above Meredith the route leads for four miles along the south shore of *Waukawan Lake*.

RAGGED MOUNTAIN & LONG POND, MEREDITH, N.H.
Boston, Concord, and Montreal R. R.

Long Pond on the right is the next body of water passed, the train gliding safely under the shadow of *Ragged Mountain*, whose rocky sides have been blasted away to give passage to the cars. This scenery and that around *Ashland* is very fine; and many a tourist artistically inclined will be lured from the cars to visit it. The *Pemigewasset* and *Squam* Rivers, which unite here, furnish many landscape "bits" of artistic beauty. The course of *Squam River* is not along our route; but the lover of the beautiful who would follow it three miles, to its source in *Squam Lake*, will be amply repaid.

Squam Lake has already been alluded to in a visit from Centre Harbor; but no single description can exhaust its picturesque beauties. Indeed, this whole region possesses peculiar charms for the liberated citizen of our larger towns, where weeks or months may be quietly spent; and, if he makes up his mind in advance to take the accommodations as he finds them, he cannot fail to be pleased. Unfortunately, no large hotel has yet been built here;

On entering the Pemigewasset Valley at Plymouth, the scenery assumes beautiful combinations of lines, and scenic effects. The whole region, both on the river and inland, is made up of grand panoramic views or choice "bits," from which the artist readily fills his sketch-book.

Engraved expressly for "Bachelder's Popular Resorts, and How to Reach Them."

PLYMOUTH, N.H.

1. Franconia Mountains.
2. Pemigewasset House.
3. Boston, Concord, & Montreal R.R.
4. Pemigewasset River.

but it is but a short drive from Centre Harbor, where all the quiet comforts of home will be found.

Ashland was formerly known as *Holderness*, and is remembered by members of the Episcopal denomination as one of the first places where that society flourished in this part of the State. Above Ashland we enter the valley of the *Pemigewasset*, which we follow to *Plymouth*.

The stranger will be particularly struck by the purity of the water in the wayside streams flowing from springs on the mountain sides. They furnish admirable nurseries for the speckled trout with which they generally abound.

The approach to Plymouth is very picturesque. The line of the road is along the banks of the river, which meanders its course through rich meadows, shaded here and there by broad-sweeping elms. On either side are high wooded hills, which, by gentle grade, sweep down to the

PEMIGEWASSET HOUSE.

valley below; while beyond in the blue distance are the *Franconia Mountains*. As you are whirled rapidly into the town, the **Pemigewasset House**, which in the distance seemed a mere speck among the trees, rises invitingly before you.

On reaching town, the train stops immediately in rear of the hotel; and, with an evident knowledge of the good things within, the passengers soon fill the long dining-rooms of the house, or the restaurants attached to it. Ample time is given for dinner, full thirty minutes, before the conductor cries, "All aboard!" But here we find that many of our companions have left us, though the number is made good by others, who have been spending a few days at this enjoyable place. *Plymouth* is deservedly one of the most popular resorts in New Hampshire. It is a compact village, with several fine churches, schools, county buildings, railroad offices, &c. But tourists visit Plymouth for its delightful surroundings, pleasant drives, and magnificent scenery, and no less for the popularity of its noble hotel, the **Pemigewasset House.**

This elegant and spacious hotel is delightfully situated on the banks of the Pemigewasset, near its confluence with Baker's River. The halls, parlors, and dining-rooms are large, light, and handsomely furnished. The chambers are high and well-ventilated. There are bath-rooms with hot and cold water, and all the modern conveniences of a first-class house. It is under the patronage of the Boston, Concord, and Montreal Railroad, and is frequented by persons of culture and taste, some having secured rooms for nine consecutive years. An air of refinement pervades its atmosphere, which is immediately *felt* by visitors.

LIVERMORE FALLS, PLYMOUTH, N.H.
Boston, Concord, and Montreal R.R.

LIVERMORE FALLS are on a wild turbid stream, which forces its way along a rugged bed of shattered rocks. The road-way crosses by a light, airy bridge immediately below the falls, affording an opportunity to view them without leaving the carriage. Where there are so many pleasant drives as in the vicinity of Plymouth, it is difficult to particularize; indeed, with the fine turn-outs furnished at the hotel, one can scarcely go amiss. The drive around *Plymouth Mt.* is very highly spoken of; and a longer excursion by private conveyance up the valley of the Pemigewasset to *Franconia Notch* is delightful.

Mount Prospect is much visited. A carriage-road leads to its summit, which is 2,963 feet above the sea. It commands a landscape view of rare beauty, embracing the Franconia and White Mountains, and this entire lake-region, of which *Winnepesaukee* is the most noted. There are also several elevations in the immediate neighborhood of the village, which pedestrians will delight to visit.

STAGE-ROUTE FROM PLYMOUTH TO THE FRANCONIA MOUNTAINS.

There are those who would find their visit to the mountains unsatisfactory without a stage-ride: to such the writer can recommend the route from *Plymouth* to the **Profile House.** It is over a good road, and through one of the most picturesque regions of New Hampshire. Artists do not generally spend their summers at the mountain-houses, but select some desirable field for their labors. The route from Plymouth to the Profile House passes through *Compton* and *Woodstock*, which is emphatically a *field for artists*, where, through the months of summer and autumn they gather the choice *bits* which occupy their winter months, and delight their friends at home. A more interesting drive can scarcely be conceived. The road passes near the *Flume*. This is a wonderful freak of nature,—an upright fissure in the rocks, which have been forced asunder by some mighty convulsion; while high up their sides is held in unyielding grasp a huge bowlder, beneath which a wild mountain torrent dashes its feathery spray. The *Pool* is a curiosity scarcely less interesting, and should be visited by the tourist. An impetuous stream, shaded by forest trees, walled in by precipitous ledges, escaping from the thicket above, leaps from the rocks into the deepening gloom below. The *Basin* is passed at the road-side, and is an exceedingly attractive feature. Here a mountain torrent rushes obliquely into a rocky caldron, around which for ages past the waters with dizzy whirl have polished its granite sides. The *Old Man* of the *Mountain* is seen on the left a half mile before reaching the **Profile House**; and it is better to visit it late in the afternoon, with the bright sky behind it. It requires no stretch of the imagination to detect the cold, sharp outline of the human profile chiselled in colossal proportions by the hand of nature. This is unquestionably the most remarkable natural curiosity in this country, if not in the world. The likeness is formed of three blocks of granite, high up the mountain-side, located rods apart; yet when viewed from *one* particular spot the profile is perfect. It is 70 feet from chin to forehead; yet the lines are softened by distance. The beautiful lake at the foot of the mountain is known as the *Old Man's Washbowl*. *Echo Lake*, near the **Profile House,** is also one of the points of interest.

The ascent of *Mt. Lafayette* is made from here, and is scarcely less interesting than that of Mt. Washington, although much more difficult and fatiguing, as it must be done on horseback, unless the tourist is a good pedestrian. This locality can also be visited with a quarter-part the stage-coach ride by keeping the cars to Littleton. Resuming our seats in the cars at Plymouth, the train for twenty miles continues up the valley of *Baker's River*. There is nothing striking in the scenery;

but the mountains and river present varied combinations of forms in which the tourist will not fail to be interested. In the vicinity of *Warren* the mountains become bolder and more rugged; and the time is not far distant when this locality will be largely frequented by lovers of fine scenery. Even now the small hotel in the village, and many private boarding-houses, are well patronized. A wild mountain

OWL'S HEAD AND MOOSILAUKE, WARREN, N.H.
Boston, Concord, and Montreal R.R.

stream in the suburbs has several waterfalls and pretty cascades, which are well worth visiting. A good carriage-road leads to the summit of *Moosilauke*, five miles away. This mountain is 4,600 feet high, and commands a magnificent prospect. Visitors will find accommodations at the **Summit House.** A fine view of *Moosilauke* may be had from the right of the cars, while going northward. A few miles above

Engraved expressly for "Bachelder's Popular Resorts, and How to Reach Them."

LITTLETON, N.H.

1. Oak Hill House.
2. High School.
3. Ammonoosuc River.
4. Mount Washington.
5. Boston, Concord, and Montreal R.R.

Warren, is a high barren cliff, called *Owl's Head*, which rises precipitously above the surrounding forests. This locality presents many points of interest, particularly for a pedestrian, who, with fishing-tackle or gun, may while away a few weeks in autumn.

The rugged form of *Owl's Head*, combined with *Moosilauke*, and the green meadows which surround them, make a beautiful landscape. Indeed, the scenery is all fine along this section of the route. *Haverhill*, a few miles farther on, is a pleasant village; the public buildings of Grafton County are located here. The line of the road has led us gradually towards the *Connecticut*. On our left are the rich bottoms which skirt its borders; and the thriving village of *Newbury, Vt.*, can be seen across the river.

The train crosses the *Connecticut* at *Woodsville* to *Wells River*, where connection is made with the Passumpsic, Montpelier, and Wells River Railroads. After receiving their White Mountain passengers, the cars re-cross to the east bank, and continue up the *Ammonoosuc*. This is indeed a pleasing stream. Its course is broken by falls and rapids; and its waters are swept by the branches of overhanging trees. The next village passed is *Bath*, which is charmingly situated on the bank of the river, and presents a very picturesque appearance. *Lisbon* is but a few miles farther on. This is a very interesting village, and pleasantly located. The discovery of a gold mine here has given it additional interest.

Littleton is the largest and most populous village in this section of the State. It contains several hotels and boarding-houses, among which **Thayer's** is the best known. The scenery at *Littleton* presents many artistic combinations. The village is built mostly on the right bank of the river, extending up the hillside. From the upper portion of the town is had an excellent view of the *White Mountains*, flanked by the *Franconia Mountains*, and other ranges equally interesting.

Littleton contains about 2500 inhabitants, and is well supplied with churches, schools, banks, and printing-offices. Indeed, it seems a miniature city, yet so small that ten minutes' walk in any direction will take you into the delightful suburbs, where all the pleasures and amusements of the country may be enjoyed. During the summer months the number of inhabitants is largely increased. The atmosphere is exhilarating, and the water pure, for which so many come heree, wher more home comforts can be enjoyed, in preference to going to the mountain-houses. From Littleton, tourists can easily visit the more important points of interest. *Mount Washington*, the *White Mountain-Notch*, *Pool*, *Flume*, *Profile*, and many other interesting places, can be visited in a day, and return the same night. Stages to the *Profile House* and *Franconia Mountains* leave here twice daily. No tourist to the mountains can afford to pass the *Franconia Notch*, without a call. Indeed, it is one of the few

Engraved expressly for Eastelder's Popular Resorts, and How to Reach Them.

LANCASTER, N.H.

1. Lunenburg Heights.
2. Connecticut River.
3. Boston, Concord, & Montreal R R
4. Lancaster House
5. Mount Lyon
6. Stratford Peaks

places where the traveller lingers. The **Profile House**, near the Notch, is one of the largest and best appointed in New England.

Seven miles above Littleton the *Wing Road* branches to the right, and continues past *Bethlehem* and **Twin Mountain House** to the **Fabyan Hotel** at the foot of Mount Washington.

The next station of importance on the main line is *Whitefield*, extensively known for its lumber operations, but more recently as a summer-resort. In the neighborhood are some fine views of mountain scenery; and the place is fast growing in popularity, which may also be said of *Dalton*, the next station on the line.

Lancaster is one of the most beautiful villages in Northern New Hampshire. It is well laid out, has concrete walks, and fine shade-

LANCASTER HOUSE,
Lancaster, N.H.

trees ornament its streets. The architecture is good; and tasteful gardens are everywhere to be seen. There are six churches, a public library, and other public buildings; and throughout the town pervades an air of taste and refinement. The village is built in an immense amphitheatre, surrounded by hills and mountains, which are reached by excellent roads, affording some of the most delightful drives in the State. The view from *Lunenburg Hills, Vt.*, is unsurpassed. Israel's River passes through, and the Connecticut near the town. There are several hotels, the most prominent being the **Lancaster House**.

The **Lancaster House** is superior to most houses situated so far from the centres of trade. It accommodates conveniently 150 guests.

The rooms are large and high-posted. From the ample cupola which surmounts it, the view of the *White Mountain Range*, *Stratford Peaks*, *Starr King*, *Pilot Range*, *Mt. Lyon*, and the green hills of Vermont, is unsurpassed. Parlor-cars run through the village from Canada, Boston, Fall River, Newport, New London, and Worcester. Lancaster is a town well calculated to please the visitor who would make it his home during the summer or autumn months.

The Waumbec House is but eight miles away, and can be reached by stage. This and other houses in *Jefferson* are in a romantic locality, which will well repay a visit.

From Lancaster the train continues to *Northumberland*, where connection is made with the Grand Trunk Railroad for *Canada* and the West.

Resuming our route on the Wing Road (see page 111), we follow up the

RAILROAD STATION, BETHLEHEM, N.H.
Boston, Concord, and Montreal R.R.

banks of the *Ammonoosuc*; though for several miles there is nothing in the character of the scenery to indicate to the tourist that he is rapidly approaching one of the most celebrated summer-resorts in America.

Bethlehem Station is the first stopping-place. The village of *Bethlehem*, two miles from the station, is one of the favorite summer residences in the mountain-region. With the increasing popularity of White Mountain travel come large numbers as sight-seers and pleasure-seekers; still, there are many who visit the highlands of New Hampshire for the water pure from its mountain springs, and fine invigorating atmosphere which sweeps the hills, and after a few months' sojourn feel that they have renewed their lease of life. The extent of country thus visited occupies an area of more than 500 square miles, embracing every variety of surface and surroundings, from the green meadow, the rolling upland, the high mountain-peak, to the dense primeval forest. The village of Bethlehem is built on a plateau or ridge of deep, rich soil, which connects the White and Franconia ranges of mountains, and commands striking views of both. *Its altitude is greater than that of any other village east of the Rocky Mountains.*

Some years ago a Boston merchant, overtaxed by business cares, and suffering from loss of health, was recommended to try a season at Bethlehem. He returned in the autumn well, — completely invigorated and restored; but each season finds him with his family at their mountain home. Thankful for this marvellous and unexpected restoration, with his ample means he determined to prepare accommo-

MAPLEWOOD HOUSE
Bethlenem, N.H.

dations where others could have the comforts of home without the expense of fitting up an establishment of their own.

A valuable farm of five hundred acres was purchased, and thoroughly stocked with improved breeds of horses, cows, and sheep, and large numbers of poultry of the most approved kinds; while the house was enlarged and placed in perfect repair, bowling and billiard saloons erected, and other games and amusements improvised for the entertainment of guests. The farm was placed under the charge of a competent person, for whom a commodious farm-house, barns, dairies, stables, and extensive out-buildings, were erected. From this farm guests are daily supplied, during the summer, with the *very best of every thing* fresh from the fields. Green corn, peas, beans, and garden-sauce, growing at one hour, are bountifully served upon the table the next. Fresh cream, butter, and eggs, of home production, are served, not at fabulous hotel-prices, but at fair and reasonable rates.

The verandas at the **Maplewood** are shaded; and the grounds are ornamented by a fine growth of sugar-maple, forming delightful playgrounds for children, and a cool and cleanly out-of-doors resort for adults.

One of the finest and most picturesque views of *Mount Washington*, and others of the White-Mountain group, is from the veranda of this house; while the vicinity abounds in delightful drives. The admirable drainage renders this a healthy and desirable residence.

From the station at Bethlehem the train continues along the bank of the *Ammonoosuc* to the **Twin Mountain House** and to the **Fabyan House**, at the base of *Mount Washington*. The **Twin Mountain House** until the present season was the terminus of the railroad. It has been extensively patronized, and will be pleasantly remembered by its patrons, as a most free and social summer home.

The buildings of this extensive summer resort were erected and furnished new in 1869-70, on a spot long occupied as a hotel, and popular with the public. The vicinity not only commands fine and varied views of the White and Franconia Mountains, but has better facilities for water amusements than any hotel of the mountain region. The house stands high on a commanding bluff, which overlooks the *Ammonoosuc*. So near its head, this stream is not usually suitable for boating; but here it is held by a dam, thus affording an admirable opportunity for that healthful and fascinating amusement. The water is fringed with trees of most delicate foliage, among which guests have constructed rural seats and arbors. This is a romantic spot, where lovers and those socially inclined do love to congregate. The forests about the "Twin Mountain" are very charming, and the shrubs and ferns fresh and varied. But the chief and practical excellence of this locality is in the entire absence of hay-fever, that disagreeable disease indigenous to so large a portion of the country. The following extract from "The New York Ledger" is from the pen of the Rev. Henry Ward Beecher, who has long been afflicted with this distressing malady, and who now spends his summer and autumn months at this health-giving place: "Meanwhile another year warrants me in saying that a resort hither is almost certain relief; not one per cent of patients failing to obtain essential if not entire relief. We can go out into the sun, stand in mud morning and evening, and in spite of dust, rain, or chill, we are well. *Laus Deo!*"

When we assert that the proprietors of this house supply every thing

TWIN-MOUNTAIN HOUSE.
Boston, Concord, and Montreal R.R.

1. Ammonoosuc River.   2. White Mountain Range.

necessary to promote the comfort, convenience, and amusement of guests, — to facilitate their movements from place to place, — it will be unnecessary to enumerate. The Boston, Concord, and Montreal Railroad has been extended the present season to the *Fabyan House.*

Carriages are in waiting on the arrival of trains to convey tourists to the Mount Washington Railway Depot, a few miles distant; and those who desire can sleep at the **Mount Washington Summit House,** on the top of the mountain, although guests generally prefer to spend the night, and longer if they choose, at the "Fabyan." The scenery is much finer while ascending the mountain on that side in the morning, while the sun is in the east, than it is in the evening, when it will shine directly in the eyes. Those who start in the morning have the additional advantage of choosing a fair day, a great *desideratum*, as it frequently rains at the summit when it is fair below. Indeed, this important advantage will always make the Fabyan the popular stopping-place; for those who wish to ascend Mount Washington but once could then be certain of a pleasant day, as the summit is distinctly seen from the door of the hotel.

The Fabyan House has been located at the intersection of the Boston, Concord, and Montreal, and the Portland and Ogdensburg Railroads with the Mount Washington Turnpike; and all persons ascending by rail, from whatever house, must first come to this point.

Since public attention was first directed to the White Mountains, the locality of the **Fabyan House** has always been popular. More than seventy years ago a tavern was built near the site of the present house, which was burned in 1819; it was soon rebuilt, however; but the second house subsequently shared the same fate. In later years, as travel has increased the demand, other houses have sprung up in different localities. These have been enlarged from time to time, to supply the wants of travel. All have points of excellence in their location; many of them comfortably accommodating a large number of guests, and the tables of all are amply supplied.

The early completion of the Boston, Concord, and Montreal Railroad, and the rapid progress of the Portland and Ogdensburg (the remaining twelve miles to be finished in 1875), with a desire to meet the demands of mountain-travel, determined a few gentlemen to erect a hotel which should compare with other large establishments of the country, — a house with large, high-studded rooms, broad halls and stairways, ample parlors, drawing-rooms, and corridors, — in a word, a structure worthy of being called a first-class hotel, and recognized as such by the travelling public. The want of such a building at the mountains has long been felt. There were already many houses where good and abundant accommodations could be had, but nothing before this which in town would be called first-class.

The present **Fabyan House** was built in the form of the letter T inverted, thus: ⊥. The top of the letter represents the main building, which is three hundred and twenty feet long by forty-five feet wide. In the centre is a rotunda sixty feet square, which is gained by projections front and back from the main building. This rotunda forms a very attractive feature, and is the common *rendezvous* of guests. The hotel and telegraph offices occupy two of its corners: from a third leads a broad, massive stairway to the two stories above.

The parlor, which is one hundred by forty-five feet, occupies the entire eastern end of the building, and is very handsomely furnished. The remainder of the ground-floor is occupied by reception and reading rooms, and private parlors, each thirty by twenty feet. From the rear centre of the rotunda extends an ell in which is the dining-room, one hundred and thirty by forty-five feet, seating comfortably four hundred guests. Carving and serving rooms, culinary offices, and kitchens, arranged with all modern appliances, are located in the rear wings of the building. There are two hundred and fifty sleeping-rooms, high, airy, light, and newly and handsomely furnished. The entire house is lighted by gas, and warmed by steam. It has billiard and bath rooms, an excellent livery, and the complete conveniences of first-class hotels.

The present site was selected for various reasons: first, for the acknowledged beauty of its surroundings, and the admirable prospect of the White-Mountain Range, a most complete view of which may be had from the veranda, — indeed, the summit of Mount Washington is but seven and a half miles distant as the bee flies; the cars can be seen with the naked eye, ascending and descending; the house on the summit is a distinctive feature; and, with a glass, visitors to the mountain can be seen skipping over the rocks. As the Fabyan House faces the north, its main veranda is always in shadow, beneath whose cooling shade, in the hottest day, a refreshing breeze is felt. To watch the cloud-shadows creep along the mountain's base, climb quickly up their rugged sides, now lingering for a moment on some projecting cliff, then clear at a single bound the deep abyss, and steal away in the distance, is a pastime ever changing, ever new, and one which never tires.

The location of the house is such as to afford front rooms to all who come to see the mountains; for it is surrounded by them in the most beautiful combinations. Those at the south are not oppressively near; but, lying beyond the babbling waters of the **Ammonoosuc**, which winds in serpentine course through the broad green meadows of the neighborhood, they raise their massive forms.

At the north a small but picturesque mountain, *Mount Prospect*, rises from the very doors. To climb this is one of the popular amusements of guests. From its sides and summit are charming views of the valley, and

Engraved expressly for Bachelder's Popular Resorts, and How to Reach Them.

FABYAN HOUSE.

1. White Mountain Range.
2. Mount Washington Turnpike.
3. Ammonoosuc River.
4. "Notch."

a more distant prospect of the **White Mountain Notch**. But the most imposing scene is the view of Mount Washington itself, flanked by others scarcely less interesting.

The following table shows how centrally and conveniently this house is situated for visiting the more prominent mountain localities, — a fact which must always make it popular for those who wish to make this a general stopping-place during a prolonged stay.

Fabyan House to Mount Washington Railway Depot	6	Miles.
" Summit of Mount Washington	9	"
" Ammonoosuc Falls	2½	"
" Mount Willard	5	"
" Waumbec House	11	"
" Profile "	22	"
" Glen "	17	"
" Crawford "	5	"
" Willey "	6½	"
" Twin-Mountain House	4	"
" Bethlehem	17	"
" Lancaster	18	"
" North Conway	25	"
" White Mountain "Notch,"	6	"
" Silver Cascade	6½	"
" Gibbs' Falls	5	"
" Beecher's Falls	5	"

The depot of the Mount Washington Railway, six miles distant from the "Fabyan," is reached by carriages for every train.

There are many points of interest in the vicinity; and the drives to them form a fine source of amusement. It is but six miles to the famous **White Mountain Notch**, and one mile farther to the **Silver Cascade**. Here a small silvery stream springs by successive leaps from the mountain top to the valley below, and like a frightened fawn darts away in the distance. The locality of the famous "Willey Slide" is a mile farther down the valley. Although many years have passed since that fearful night, time has failed to heal the wounds it made. The house still stands; and the spot where the family was buried is pointed out to visitors. **Mount Willard** is in this neighborhood, to whose summit a fine carriage-road has been built. The view from Mount Willard is grand, embracing the **Willey Notch** in the foreground, and stretching away into the blue distance. These objects are all in the vicinity of the **Crawford House**, which is but five miles from the Fabyan, and has for many years been one of the most popular houses in the mountains. **Gibbs' Falls, Beecher's Falls,** and other points of interest, are also in this neighborhood. Indeed, these interesting natural features are entitled to something more than a passing notice from the writer, or a casual glance from the tourist; and those who would study them can best do so from the Crawford House.

For the lover of the wild and picturesque, the tourist will find ample opportunities to gratify his taste by a visit to Gibbs Falls, particularly if the stream is traced to its source at the base of the mountains. This locality was examined and the falls sketched by the writer in 1857, and named for the (then) proprietor of the Crawford House. Beecher's Falls have been popularized by the interest taken in them by their noted namesake.

The "Notch" is the great natural gateway to the White Mountains proper. Mounts Webster and Willard form its outstanding pillars. The scenery is grander than by any other approach. Nowhere can this be so well realized as from the summit of Mount Willard, which, with its admirable carriage-way, must always be one of the most popular resorts in this region. The "Gate of the Notch," flanked by perpendicular ledges, is but twenty-four feet wide; through which passes the carriage-road, and flow the waters of the *Saco*, which rises a short distance above. The *Crawford House* is also the starting-point of the only bridle-path to Mount Washington, which no person physically able should fail to visit. The path enters the forest at the house, through which it winds its way by a rough course to the summit of Mount Clinton; thence continuing by a rugged pathway over (or around) Mount Pleasant, Mount Franklin, Mount Monroe, to Mount Washington. The route follows the crest of the mountains, and affords a combination of the finest views in the region, — one of the grandest of which embraces that stupendous gulf, **Tuckerman's Ravine**, which falls sheer down a thousand feet. This not only forms one of the wildest retreats about the mountains, but it generally contains an individual feature of interest, the snow-arch. During the winter months, the north-west winds completely fill this chasm with snow, which, packed by the driving storms of wind and sleet, by the warm rains of spring and the hot sun of summer, settles to a firm, compact mass. As the swollen streams pass beneath, the snow is melted. The massive bowlders which fill the valley become the base of so many ice-pillars, which remain and uphold the enormous snow-arch above. On the 12th of August, 1857, the writer entered this cavern to the distance of three hundred feet, and, by estimate, found the snow still twenty-five feet thick. It all passes away, however, by the last of August or the first of September. Tuckerman's Ravine can be visited from the Summit or from the Glen House.

The bridle-path excursion, about nine miles, is frequently made by pedestrians. But no one should attempt it without being well shod; and the sudden accumulation of clouds and mists on the mountains renders an experienced guide indispensable. The "Crawford" has always been noted for its admirable *cuisine*, and will be found withal one of the most desirable houses at the mountains. It is also reached by stage by the North Conway route, from the terminus of the Portland and Ogdensburg Railroad. This approach is grand; and the mountain combinations are picturesque and beautiful. The stage-ride is an enjoyable feature. The road passes the Willey House, Silver Cascade, Flume, and debouches from the mountains at the Gate of the Notch. Stages connect with all prominent Houses, and with the Mount Washington Railway, via Fabyan House.

The stage-ride from the Crawford and Fabyan Houses to the Mount Washington Railway Station is one of the most exciting features of mountain travel.

AMMONOOSUC FALLS.

The falls of the Ammonoosuc are passed by the wayside, and are well worth a visit. Here the rocks have been worn by the action of the water into a thousand fantastic forms. The road leads through a primeval forest: luxuriant vines laden with fruit and berries spring from the virgin soil, often tempting the visitor from the carriage. We occasionally catch a glimpse of the grand old mountain, as it raises its granite head above the clouds. The ascent of Mount Washington was once a feat of rare occurrence, accomplished only by the daring hunter or adventurous traveller; but the industry and perseverance of man have smoothed the way; and the route has been made easy, safe, and pleasant.

To accompany an aëronaut, to look out upon the surrounding world, has been the desire of many, though enjoyed by few. Here the "iron horse," guided by the hand of genius, climbs triumphantly to the dizzy height of 6,285 feet, more than a mile in the air, where the "storm-king," riding on the wings of the whirlwind, have hitherto reigned supreme; and yet all this is done in absolute safety, and with as much ease as the same distance could be accomplished over any road in the country.

The ascent should be made the subject of some preparation. To attempt it improperly clothed would risk the pleasure of the excursion. You *may* not meet a snow storm, or find icicles hanging from the roof in the morning; but you are *liable* to any month in the year. Ladies, particularly, should not rely upon a shawl alone for protection, but add a full suit of winter extra under-clothing. You will find the house on the summit heated by steam, and a cheerful fire in the grate; but you should not, for want of proper clothing, lose the opportunity for out-of-door pleasures.

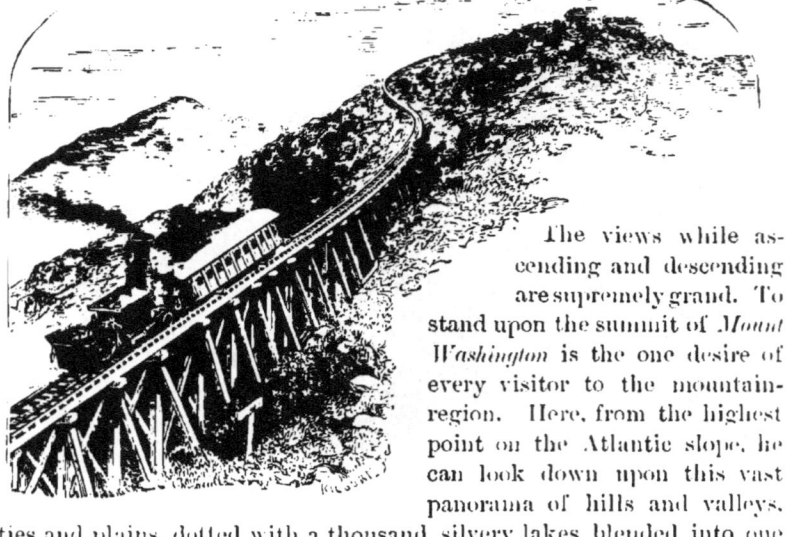

The views while ascending and descending are supremely grand. To stand upon the summit of *Mount Washington* is the one desire of every visitor to the mountain-region. Here, from the highest point on the Atlantic slope, he can look down upon this vast panorama of hills and valleys, cities and plains, dotted with a thousand silvery lakes blended into one harmonious whole. Without putting foot upon the ground, he is lifted step by step up this rugged steep, to the very doors of the Hotel, which, bound with chains to the barren cliff, has been built and furnished to receive him.

The **Mount Washington Summit House** accommodates conveniently one hundred and seventy-five guests, though more than two hundred have been entertained. Several thousand persons visited it during the past season. Its appointments are very complete. Lighted by gas, and heated by steam, with all modern improvements, a liberal table, and good attendance, the visitor can be made comfortable for any length of time. Stages run from the railroad depot to all the prominent houses, enabling tourists to return by any route they choose.

Richfield Springs. — "These springs, long and favorably known, are in Otsego County, N.Y., in the vicinity of Cooperstown, and seven miles distant from Otsego Lake, which is one of the sources of the Susquehanna. The great river of Pennsylvania here extends his arms and intwines his fingers with the tributaries of the Mohawk, as if to divert that gentle river from its allegiance to the Hudson. The village of Richfield Springs is situated upon a narrow plain, near the head of **Schuyler's Lake,** which is five miles in length, and a mile and a quarter at its greatest breadth. This little lake is surrounded with high hills on every side, except the northward; and, being but a mile from the springs, forms the principal attraction for visitors. According to tradition, the waters of these springs were sought, for their medicinal virtues, by the Indians, long before the advent of the white men. A healing prophet of the Iroquois dwelt on an island in the midst of the lake; and the suffering came to him, to be cured by the waters he secured at night and conveyed secretly to his retreat. But the Great Spirit became angered at his pride, and sunk him and his island beneath the deep waters."

Glen's Falls, N.Y., so graphically pictured in Cooper's novel, "The Last of the Mohicans," are on the railroad from Saratoga, and are scarcely excelled, for fierce and turbulent grandeur, by any body of angered waters in the country. They are well worth a few days of pause and study, on the way to

Nahant, Mass., is among the mature celebrities of the New England coast. It is one of those rare combinations of natural and remarkable beauties which assert their superiority without the need of art or special praise. Yet Nahant is a lesson. It teaches the fickleness of human fancy, and the uncertainty of popular favor. If this really charming spot were only located a hundred or more miles from the leading marts of New England trade, it would scarce find a rival in fashionable and public approval. It is too near Boston and other cities, too easy of access, and too comfortable generally, to attract the great multitude; who prove that "distance lends enchantment to the view" of a summer trip and life, by seeking remote and out-of-the-way places in preference. Yet Nahant is so delightfully located, so varied in its scenery and surroundings, so dotted with wonderful curiosities of nature, so graced with romantic and ever-varying specialties, and so readily reached, that the number of its summer residents and brief visitors will ever be very large. It was the chief resort of the wealthy and the gay only a few years since; but the worshippers of fashion now travel to other shrines. It is still the abode of many wealthy and distinguished characters during the hot season, and is easily visited by steamers from Boston, and by the "Eastern Railroad" *viâ* Lynn.

Lake George. — "Few, if any, among the numerous picturesque lakes in America are more beautiful or more celebrated than this, which lies between the Counties of Washington and Warren, in the State of New York, and is thirty-six miles long, varying in breadth from three-quarters of a mile to four miles, and in many places is four hundred feet in depth. It is in the midst of mountains; and popular belief credits it with islands equal in number to the days of the year. History, as well as tradition, lingers around it, marking many spots with more than ordinary interest. Not the least among these are the ruins of Fort William Henry and Fort George. Sir William Johnson, prompted by his loyalty, named it Lake George, after one of the Georges of Great Britain; and this title has been permitted to remain as its designation. A writer, describing the many attractions of the lake, says, 'It has something of interest for every one, — the lover of history, of romance, of beauty, and lovers generally.'"

The Glen is one of the largest summer resorts in the White Mountain region. This fine establishment occupies a most picturesque location in the beautiful valley of the Peabody River, within a few rods of Mount Washington Summit Carriage-Road (which is one of the best constructed roads in the country), commanding a fine view, from base to summit, of Mounts Washington, Jefferson, Adams, and Madison, head of Tuckerman Ravine, and the Carter Range, — forming one of the finest panoramas to be obtained in the whole mountain region of New Hampshire.

Other points of especial interest in the vicinity are Glen Ellis Falls, Crystal Cascade, &c.

The access to the Glen is by stages from the "Grand Trunk" Railway, at Gorham, Me., and from the "Portland and Ogdensburg," and "Eastern," at Bartlett, N.H.

York Beach, Me., and, beyond that, **Bald Head Cliff**, — a wild, stern, defiant-fist rock, in almost constant battle with the waves of the sea, — are places of interest, and when better known will command their share of patronage. The run to these points can be made from Portsmouth.

Watch Hill Point, R.I., has a good local popularity. Its high, commanding location, and extended prospect and fine beaches, must eventually, when better known, bring it into more general favor. It commands a fine view of Long Island Sound. Watch Hill, like Narraganset Pier, is dependent upon boat transportation. Steamboats run from Norwich, Mystic, and New London, Conn., and Stonington, Westerly, R.I.

THE PENNSYLVANIA RAILROAD.

THE Pennsylvania Railroad may well be said to stand at the head of the railway system of America. Like the aorta of the human body, which connects the heart with other important organs, thence ramifying into the extremities, this road, with its branches and connections, forms the *great central line of the country.* It not only extends a greater number of

COATESVILLE BRIDGE.

miles, uses more running stock, and employs more men, than any other, but in point of construction it is considered the *model* railroad of the United States. The bridges alone, in the scientific knowledge and artistic beauty displayed in their construction, would form an exhaustive subject for description. The Coatesville Bridge, at the village of Coatesville, is a beautiful and imposing structure. It stretches eight hundred and fifty feet across a chasm, and is seventy-five feet high. Like many of the bridges along this road, it is built of iron supported by stone pillars, thus securing strength and durability with architectural beauty combined. Indeed, this is a distinctive feature of the Pennsylvania Railroad; and throughout the entire line no expense is spared in the construction of bridges and culverts.

CONNECTING RAILROAD BRIDGE,
Fairmount Park, Philadelphia.

"So far as scenery goes, no lines of railroad on the continent can surpass those running through Pennsylvania. Magnificent agricultural panoramas, beautiful river views, splendid mountain pictures, picturesque hills and valleys, lovely villages, and flourishing towns and cities, are seen in quick succession. A ride of twelve hours between Philadelphia and Pittsburg shows more interesting variety than can be seen in the same time and distance anywhere else in the United States.

"On, on, on, goes this tireless train, over a clear track, carrying the traveller by a panorama, the like of which can be found nowhere else on this continent, and probably not in the world. After having breakfasted in the Mississippi Valley, and dined at the capital of Pennsylvania, the passenger finds himself seated at supper in the metropolis of New York, where the Atlantic throbs and swells in its ceaseless activity.

"It is no new thing to say that the scenery on the line of the Pennsylvania road is beautiful, and in many places grand. Every American who travels or reads has seen or heard of it; and the pencils of many artists have labored lovingly to portray, for popular gratification, the attractions of the Alleghany mountains; the Juniata, Susquehanna, and Conemaugh Rivers, and the wonderful agricultural vales of Lancaster and Chester Counties, through which this road runs. Long sweeps of wooded hills; lofty mountains and dark ravines; picturesque valleys opening into each other; sparkling and placid waters; wide, rolling, pastoral landscapes,—follow in rapid succession. The magnificent rivers are crossed by corresponding bridges. The bold mountain ranges and wild ravines, which would have disheartened a less enterprising company, are overcome by feats of engineering skill, which, combined with the natural artistic features of the country, make this the most interesting route in America.

COLUMBIA BRIDGE,
Fairmount Park, Philadelphia, Pa.

This bridge is located in a charming region. It spans the Schuylkill, which runs through Fairmount Park, connecting the east and west portions. Indeed, Philadelphia and its suburbs has an unusual number of bridges, some of them noted for their strength and beauty, while all add greatly to the interest of the scenery. The vicinity of Laurel Hill Cemetery is particularly noticeable. The bridges which span the Schuylkill make a striking foreground for the beautiful landscape beyond.

A few years ago, the man who should have predicted such improvements would have been pronounced hopelessly insane. Not even the most sanguine enthusiast on railroads, when their construction was commenced, dreamed of overcoming distance so rapidly and at such a rate; and it is only because of the perfection of machinery and the inventions of science that it can be done now.

FAIRMOUNT PARK, PHILADELPHIA.

Tourists, especially for pleasure, can scarcely find a more desirable spot for a day's enjoyment than Fairmount Park. Central Park of New York is older, and has received more artificial embellishments; but in size, or in the character of natural attractions, Fairmount has no equal in America. It contains nearly three thousand acres, — more than three times as large as Central Park. The beautiful Schuylkill flows through it, affording a great variety of fine water views, with admirable facilities for boating. In addition to this, the Wissahickon — famous for its charming, picturesque scenery — contributes six miles of leafy banks to its adornment. The Fairmount Water-works, which have been in operation since 1822; the celebrated Wire Bridge; the bronze statue of Lincoln; the mansion of Robert Morris of Revolutionary fame, once the resort of illustrious men, now fallen to decay, — are among the attractions. But nothing short of a personal visit can convey an idea of its beauties.

The charming Wissahickon of itself indelibly fixes for Fairmount Park a pre-eminence over any of its competitors. It is rare, indeed, that a city of the magnitude of Philadelphia can boast within its borders a "retreat" of such rich variety and exquisite loveliness. A more pleasing combination of the wild and picturesque, the grand and beautiful, cannot be found in America, than are presented on the banks of the Wissahickon.

HESTONVILLE, NEAR PHILADELPHIA.

Fairmount can be reached by several lines of street railway, or via Pennsylvania Railroad to Hestonville, West Philadelphia, which is three miles from the depot at Thirty-second and Market streets.

STATISTICAL DATA.

The Pennsylvania Railroad (main line) formerly extended from Philadelphia to Pittsburg, a distance of three hundred and fifty-four miles. Now it has its eastern termini at New York, Philadelphia, Baltimore, and Washington; and unites them, by its own direct lines, with Pittsburg, Erie, Cleveland, Toledo, Chicago, Cincinnati, Indianapolis, Louisville, and St. Louis. Connections are also made with St. Paul, Duluth, Omaha, Denver, the cities of California, and with Memphis, Mobile, and New Orleans.

To transact its extended and diversified business, the Company now owns, and runs upon its own lines, eleven hundred locomotives, one thousand passenger cars, and twenty-six thousand freight cars. It owns two thousand miles of completed road, besides the other thousands which it controls. Its workshops cover an area of more than five hundred acres. It employs a vast army of men, many of whom are mechanics and experts of the highest skill. It has two hundred and twenty-two foreign ticket-offices (and agents, independent of those at its own stations), established in thirteen different States. Its chief officers have been civil engineers; and they employ in their service thoroughly practical men.

It is from the proceeds of a business of such mammoth proportions that this Company are able to overcome difficulties along portions of their line, which it would be folly for a less wealthy corporation to undertake. A knowledge of these advantages induced the formation of a new organization, known as the "Pennsylvania Company," having for its object the consolidation and harmonious management of all roads under its control. This company, with a capital of $12,000,000, was organized by the election of Thomas A. Scott, Esq., as president. In 1873 it had nearly five thousand miles of railroad under its control.

CONSTRUCTION.

Ordinarily companies are satisfied if their roads are graded with sand or gravel. The Pennsylvania uses, in addition, eighteen inches of broken stone, in which the ties are embedded. This insures a dry, elastic, permanent bed, free from dust, allowing the car doors and windows to be kept open in summer. Steel rails of maximum weight are used, connected at the ends by plates, bolted to the sides, but so arranged that expansion or contraction will not cramp the rail. The joints are made *between* ties; thus insuring an agreeable elasticity, which rails secured in a "chair," *on* the ties, never have.

The Pennsylvania Railroad Company, in the construction of its road, employs the highest grade of engineering talent, and the best skilled labor; hence, although its course along the streams and through the mountains follows a tortuous route, a rate of speed can be maintained with impunity which would be actually dangerous on most roads in the country. Although the original cost of construction is much greater, the Pennsylvania Company finds it more satisfactory, and believes it to be cheaper in the end. The "stone ballast" allows the water from the heavy rains of autumn to percolate through it, leaving a dry bed for winter, and therefore free from the annoying frost upheavals, and consequent displacement of rails, as well as from the dust of summer, to which clay and gravel ballasted roads are subjected. "Jumping the track" is never known on the Pennsylvania Road. This is believed to be due to the thorough construction of its bed.

The accommodations provided for summer tourists on the line of the Pennsylvania Railroad are unsurpassed. Good hotels in all the towns reached by it are the rule, not the exception; and many of them are elegant in all their appointments. It would be difficult to select any highway of travel anywhere that can compare, in the essentials of comfort, safety, expedition, and interest, with the magnificent system of railroads managed by this Company.

It is not proposed to describe the scenery along the many branches of the Pennsylvania Railroad. Even the roads can scarcely be alluded to; and to describe and illustrate the scenery would require a volume larger than this. This cut of the Delaware Water-Gap represents one of the many resorts which its branches reach, of which a full-page cut is also annexed.

DELAWARE WATER-GAP.

The State of Pennsylvania is in itself an interesting study. Its bosom holds all the anthracite, and much of the bituminous, coal found on the continent. Its hidden fountains produce the larger portion of the oil now so essential to the comfort and industry of the world. Many of its hills are depositories of iron and other ores, which are utilized in immense factories, seen in every valley. Its forests supply the principal part of the lumber used in the great cities of the Atlantic seaboard. Its soil varies from the richest to the poorest. Its territory is washed by the tides of the Atlantic and the waters of Lake Erie, and is drained into the Gulf of Mexico by rivers navigable more than two thousand miles. Its boundaries completely separate New England and New York from the Mississippi Valley; and its entire area is dotted by scenes of more than ordinary historical interest. All these combinations add to the charm and interest of travel; and every American can find something in it instructive and gratifying.

DELAWARE WATER GAP.

The day express from Pittsburg to New York is a wonderful result of engineering skill.

This magnificent run of four hundred and forty-four miles is made with but three stoppages, — the first, of only five minutes, at Altoona, after a stretch of one hundred and seventeen miles; the second, of twenty minutes for dinner, at Harrisburg, after an unbroken dash of one hundred and thirty-two miles; and the third and last, of only five minutes, at Philadelphia, after a run of one hundred and five miles, leaving a single stretch of ninety miles across New Jersey to destination. No time being lost in stopping, the wonderful locomotive-engines work away with the regularity of fixed machinery, — *taking their supply of water from the track-tanks as they go, and carrying their fuel with them;* and the time is made by uniformity of progress more than by an increased rate of speed. The train is made up of Pullman parlor cars and the best of the Company's day coaches, all splendidly upholstered, mounted on combination springs, and furnished with plate-glass windows, through which the landscape can be distinctly seen.

But it is, perhaps, more natural to take the tourist, in imagination, from the eastern to the western termini. A description of the route from Washington and Baltimore will be found elsewhere, in an article on the Northern Central Railroad. That train joins us.

The tourist will early remark the tasteful yet substantial character of the stations on the Pennsylvania Railroad. These are usually built of stone; and for artistic effect several kinds are frequently used.

The thorough construction of the road-bed will also be noticed; the "stone ballast" and other features tending to give strength and durability to the structure. But the first peculiar *sensation* will be experienced as the train, with unabated speed, dashes around a curve in the road; and the oscillating movement of the car instinctively causes you to attempt to overcome it. But confidence soon assumes her sway; and what was at first a cause of fear becomes a source of pleasure. Chester Valley furnishes the first grand view of landscape scenery. The cars pass along an elevated ridge on the outer rim of this magnificent amphitheatre, affording a landscape of peculiar grandeur and loveliness. From Philadelphia to Lancaster the road leads through an undulating country, interspersed with fine cultivated farms, fields, and forests, while thriving villages and flourishing manufactories enliven the scene.

The Columbia Branch, which intersects the Pennsylvania Railroad at Lancaster, connects at Columbia with the York Branch, and at York with the Northern Central Railroad, affording the most direct route from Philadelphia to Gettysburg, a very popular resort.

A few minutes spent at Lancaster for refreshments, and the train is hurrying on to the banks of the Susquehanna, which we strike a short distance below Harrisburg; and until we reach that place the river is constantly in view. On the opposite banks the trains on the Northern Central Railroad, with passengers from Baltimore and Washington, can be seen.

A few miles above Harrisburg, the Pennsylvania Railroad crosses the Susquehanna over a bridge 3,845 feet long, affording an imposing view of the river and surrounding scenery. At this point the mountain barrier has been forced asunder by some mighty convulsion; and the grand old stream, having united its forces above, moves calmly on to the sea. This mountain gorge is the gate which opens to fields beyond of untold wealth and beauty. From this point, by the Northern Central and Philadelphia and Erie Railroads, on the east bank of the river, we can continue a hundred miles along this beautiful stream, with scenes ever changing ever new, and yet so beautiful that every turn presents a charming picture. Here bold, precipitous mountains, with overhanging rocks, crowd down to the river's bank, around which we quickly glide; again the hills recede to the blue distance, giving place to rich, cultivated fields and cosey farm-houses. But our course leads up the *west* bank of the Susquehanna, the most magnificent river in Pennsylvania, to the mouth of

THE BEAUTIFUL JUNIATA.

Turning up this lovely stream, whose praises have been sung by the poet's muse, we flash along its banks, around the hills, and through the valleys, catching, as we go, glimpses of picturesque villages, quiet vistas, and charming landscapes, stopping at last at Altoona.

"Altoona is situated at the head of Logan Valley, immediately at the base of the main Alleghany Mountains, and is the location of the principal construction and repair shops of the Pennsylvania Railroad Company. This Company has, in fact, created the town; and the business it concentrates here not only sustains it, but stimulates it into prosperity and rapid growth. The shops of the Company are among the most extensive and complete on the continent, and in themselves are objects of more than ordinary interest, illustrating, as they do, the perfection of American railroad management."

LOGAN HOUSE, ALTOONA, PENN.
Pennsylvania Railroad.

Southward from Altoona runs a system of branch railroads, penetrating the extensive iron deposits and rich agricultural valleys existing in Blair County. The manufacture of iron is extensively carried on all through this region, some of the establishments being large and complete. The limestone valleys are highly improved, and among the most productive in Pennsylvania. Wedged in between the eastern spurs of the Alleghanies, they are surrounded by picturesque scenery, and enjoy an atmosphere of more than ordinary purity. The streams flowing through them are fed by mountain springs, and are deliciously cool and clear, affording favorite homes for trout; and the angler finds the locality one of his paradises.

At Altoona, our sharpened appetite appeased at the **Logan House,** one of the many excellent hotels built by the Company for the accommodation of travellers, and re-enforced by an additional locomotive, with undiminished speed we dash up a grade of ninety-five feet to the mile. Bold precipices and deep chasms threaten our further course; yet up, up the mountain-side we climb,— this load of living freight, along a route which the frightened deer would have shunned a half century ago. But now our course is surely barred: high precipices tower above our heads; and the roar of a wild torrent can be heard through the mists of the deepening valley below. As we enter a gorge, the mountain flings itself in our path; but, turning to the left, on we fly. We pass the famous "Horseshoe Bend," and the race is won. By engineering skill, that charm of science, this seemingly impassable gulf is safely passed. The train soon enters a tunnel of 3,872 feet, and emerges on the western face of the mountains. We stop at "**Cresson**" the popular summer resort, near the summit of the Alleghanies, and leave the visitors to this delightful "retreat."

MOUNTAIN HOUSE, CRESSON, PENN.
Pennsylvania Railroad.

"**Cresson** — situated almost on the summit of the Alleghany Mountains, where they are crossed by the Pennsylvania Railroad, at an altitude of two thousand feet above the level of the sea — is a very popular resort during the hot months of summer.

The accommodations provided are of the best kind; the surroundings are attractive; the atmosphere is deliciously cool and pure." The primeval forests, with which the place is surrounded, are permeated by a labyrinth of paths, cosey nooks, and rustic seats. Berries of the most luxuriant growth abound; "and, in brief, it would be difficult to find a more delightful retreat from the stifling heat of cities in midsummer, than is here provided by nature and art combined. Several springs of medicinal waters flow from the mountain in the vicinity; and pleasant drives lead away through the almost unbroken forests, where the laurel spreads its wreath of blossoms in spring, and resinous hemlocks and pines give forth their aroma, and sigh their ceaseless music. The old Portage Road, with its ten inclined planes — once an American wonder, but now abandoned — crossed the mountain very near to Cresson, and in its ruins possesses great interest for all who note the advance of improvement. A short distance from the place, and accessible by stages, is **Loretto**, a centre of Catholic faith and education, founded by Father Gallitzen, a prince of the noble house of that name in Russia, who retired into this wilderness, and devoted his fortune and his life to the cause of religion."

On resuming our westward course with rapid speed, the downward grade is passed; yet the Westinghouse Air Brake controls the train, giving security to its movements, and ease and confidence to the tourist. The scenery from the Alleghanies to Pittsburg, though fine, does not compare with the remarkable combination of the beautiful, thegr and, and the sublime to be found east of the mountains.

Pittsburg is located at the junction of the Monongahela and Alleghany Rivers, the head waters of the Ohio. It commands an immense inland navigation, and possesses remarkable geographical advantages. It is situated in the heart of the bituminous coal formation; and the location of extensive beds of iron ore is equally favorable. Pittsburg is also an important railway centre, besides being one of the most thriving manufacturing cities in the Union. The scenery here is bold and striking.

The **Branch Roads** of this Company reach some of the most delightful summer resorts in the United States, and carry the traveller through scenery as beautiful as can be found on the continent. At Harrisburg connection is made with the Cumberland Valley Railroad, which passes through the lovely Cumberland and into the great Shenandoah Valley of Virginia. At Huntingdon trains are in waiting to convey visitors to the famed Bedford Springs; and at Tyrone connection is made with the Bald Eagle Valley and Clearfield Roads, which run through regions unsurpassed in picturesqueness. Indeed, as before stated, to give any thing like a connected sketch of the scenery reached by the Pennsylvania Railroad and its branches, would require a book of itself.

NEW YORK CITY AND VICINITY.

New York City does not come within the design of this work, as a place of "popular resort." It is the great cities whose tens of thousands swarm to distant places, in pursuit of rest and recreation, when the sun pours down its summer heats. Cities have their peculiar points of striking interest, distinctive of art and wealth, refinement and cultivation. These are about as well studied, in the main, at one season as at another. Nature has there been subdued; and more formal things usurp her claims. But all our notable cities have their fringes of exquisite charms, replete with luxuries and delicacies, to which the multitude make frequent resort; and from these prolific centres the pilgrims in pursuit of ease or pastime make their summer journeys. The vast suburban regions around New York present an infinite variety of nooks and resting-places free from heat and glare and city turmoil. To enumerate these in detail would be useless. If we can glance at the leading lines of inviting travel, and places for repose, the balance can all be taken in while thus upon the wing.

UP THE HUDSON.

Taking royal precedence of all rivals, commencing at the city of New York, is the **Hudson River**,—or, rather, its grand and glorious shore views. Novelty, in describing this renowned river, has long since passed out of the possible. Its panegyrists embrace the ablest pens and the most gifted minds, not to speak of the hosts who have tried and failed. Indeed, the scenery that paints the margin of the Hudson, and as far into the remote as vision can reach, simply defies the power of descriptive delineation in printer's ink. The delicate and appreciative colors of the true artist alone can exhibit the tenderness of the tints and shades; the gently serpentine lines; the valleys and verdure; the modest undula'ion; the sharp and rugged ascent; the grand and majestic mountain curves and piercing summits, with their soft haze, virgin blues, and rich, deep purples; and all these repeated, like a dream echo, in the water mirror between. It is genius only that can attempt to convey some grateful idea of how the scenery of the Hudson River fascinates and delights all minds and all grades of people, when viewed in the full glory of a robust summer. To enjoy the river to advantage, one should make the day trip, by steamer for Albany. What will be seen must be left for the reader to learn by study, as he winds along the sinuous route of the river. It will richly repay for the time and cost of the trip, as a rare painting by nature, graced by many a gem of architecture and art.

It should be borne in mind, that along the Hudson River, and at points not remote from its waters, are numerous memorable localities, where some of the sharpest conflicts and most momentous events of the Revolutionary war occurred. The holding of New York City by the British; their efforts to extend their occupation, and that of the patriots to hem them into as narrow a space as possible, — these, with the distractions which attend all like scenes, stamped the still living impress of the struggle upon many a field of strategy, skirmish, and battle. Of these, Forts Washington and Lee (both close to the city) are notable; also Fort Tryon and King's Bridge. All these spots are mentioned in histories of the Revolution, especially the desperate battle at King's Bridge, in 1777.

Yonkers is as familiar to a New Yorker as the Central Park.

The lover of old stories will find rare studies of old things around Piermont, N.Y., more especially the jail in which Major André was confined, and the spot where he was executed. These are at the ancient town of Tappan, near Piermont.

Washington Irving's home, "Sunnyside," is plainly seen on the right as you ascend the River Hudson.

Tarrytown, N.Y., where Major André was arrested, is a notable place. Cooper's graphic descriptions of the "Skinners" and "Cowboys" are laid in this region; and Irving's "Sleepy Hollow" is also close by.

Sing Sing, N.Y., is chiefly noted for its great prison and the Croton Aqueduct.

Croton Point, N.Y., holds the great lake and the vast reservoirs which supply the city of New York with water. Some of the grandest triumphs of modern engineering skill are here to be seen.

At Haverstraw, N.Y., Arnold and André met to arrange for the surrender of West Point. It is about forty miles up the river.

The famous "Stony Point," the scene of "Mad" Anthony Wayne's gallant exploit, lies just above Haverstraw, in New York State.

Peekskill, N.Y., has several Revolutionary reminiscences in its midst. On the opposite side of the river is the place where Capt. Kidd is said to have buried the treasures so much sought for, but not yet found.

Ascending Hudson River, and once past Peekskill, the grand diversities of "the Highlands" open to view, and continue to excite wonder and admiration, beyond the power of language adequately to express. These commence about fifty miles up the Hudson, and are probably unsurpassed for romantic scenery by any river travel in the Old World or in the New. To mention even the more notable, much less all the familiar features along and near this river, or to attempt a detailed description of them, would demand too much space.

West Point, the most renowned fortification on this continent, stands at the entrance to the Highland scenery of Hudson River, N.Y., and is a specially conspicuous object of interest to strangers.

Back from the Hudson River, N.Y., some dozen miles, rise the celebrated Kaatskill (more generally "Catskill") Mountains. These are full of striking objects of rare and wonderful diversity, in the study of which no intelligent person of elevated tastes can ever weary. It was in these mountains that Rip Van Winkle took his wonderful nap.

The traveller in New York State who has the leisure can reach all the more attractive places, herein mentioned, by rail or by steamer,— and guide-books, with excellent descriptions and facts, may be readily procured before commencing to "do" that region,— by starting from New York City.

VICINITY OF NEW YORK.

The objects of prominent interest within easy reach of New York are innumerable; and the demands of so vast a population must necessarily develop abundant and ready means of access to all of these.

The stupendous work at High Bridge, by which Croton water is taken over the Harlem River, is easily reached, and richly worth studying.

Trips are constantly made down the bay, from New York City, to many attractive resorts, and especially to island watering-places of much note. To all of these, throngs of every class go; but the companies assembled are not always the most orderly or choice.

Long Island, lying between the Atlantic and Long Island Sound, receives a large summer population, and is profusely provided with facilities for rambling, bathing, shooting, and fishing. The Long Island Railroad is the principal line of communication, although the Coney Island, the New York and Flushing, the Southside, and other routes, afford a wide and ready scope of access to the various resorts for pleasure-seekers.

New Lebanon Springs, of much celebrity for their medicinal properties, afford a very delightful region to visit, independent of the interest felt by invalids in the healthful waters. This place may be reached by the Harlem Road, from New York.

Few persons go to New Lebanon Springs without gratifying their curiosity by a visit to the Shaker village, two miles off, to study Shaker life.

Columbia Springs, near Hudson, is a favorite resort at all seasons, for great numbers of visitors, but in the summer more especially.

Lake George, which is a modest world of land and water beauties,— too little cultivated by hunters after charming scenery and healthful air. Lake George is a fairy land of wonderful fascinations; and the weary of body and mind, or the despondent and languid invalid, and no less the strong and healthful, will find both mind and body invigorated, and the soul elevated, by a sojourn among the picturesque beauties of that lovely lake.

EXCURSION THROUGH LONG ISLAND SOUND,

BY THE STONINGTON LINE.

NOTHING conduces so much to the pleasure of travel as a feeling of security. Whether flashing through the valleys of a beautiful landscape, around the hills, along the streams, or across the broad prairies; whether skimming the waters of some placid lake, stemming the current of a mighty river, or ploughing old "ocean's billows,"—the pleasure of the excursion will be in direct ratio to the confidence of the excursionist in the character and reliability of the route. In this particular THE STONINGTON STEAMBOAT LINE stands at the head of steam travel in America.

These boats possess the advantage of having been substantially built for outside service. They lay low in the water, presenting less surface to the winds, and in storms ride the waves "like a thing of life." They are unsurpassed for speed, comfort, and safety; and, whatever the state of the weather, *always make the trip, and are sure of connections.*

The change from the busy whirl and heated streets of a crowded city to the open harbor, where the sea-breeze sweeps unobstructed from shore to shore, is a source of great relief; and the sail from New York, through the harbor, up the East River, through Hell Gate, and down Long Island Sound, is one of the most delightful on the coast. The ferry-boats fly hither and thither like things of life. The gayly-dressed ships, bearing the fruit and merchandise of foreign climes; the forest of masts, with their streaming pennants, which for miles line the wharves along which we sail; the magnificent suburban residences and fine public buildings, with cultivated grounds, which adorn the banks; and the receding city clothed in the rich, warm glow of a beautiful sunset, — combine to make this sail one of the enjoyable episodes of a pleasant tour. THIS IS THE GREAT INSIDE LINE, leaving New York every afternoon (Sundays excepted) from Pier 33, North River, at 5, P.M., in summer, and 4 in winter, and continuing to Boston *via* Stonington, entirely avoiding Point Judith, a dangerous promontory, against which, during storms, the waves dash with fearful violence, making the passage, if not always dangerous, at least unpleasant to persons unaccustomed to sea-life.

The **Providence Railroad**, by which passengers from the boat continue to Boston, is one of the best appointed in the country. Its *Chair Cars* are a great luxury, and add much to the comfort of tourists.

THE STONINGTON LINE POSSESSES ANOTHER IMPORTANT ADVANTAGE.

Should any detention of the cars, or the probability of a rough or foggy night on the Sound, render such a course desirable, passengers from Boston for New York can change cars before reaching the boat, and continue on the SHORE LINE by rail, thus insuring Southern or Western connections in New York.

DAY-BOAT.

The *Stonington Line* has built and magnificently furnished a splendid boat, of 3,000 tons burthen, **The Rhode Island**, Capt. Jones, which will leave Pier 30 North River, at the foot of Chambers Street, at 12 o'clock, noon, and Pier at the foot of 23d Street, East River, at 1, P.M., affording passengers the unequalled privilege of a sail through Long Island Sound by daylight, arriving in Boston, at the Providence Depot, the same evening. No person who has not experienced it can conceive of the grateful change of atmosphere from a heated city, or dusty cars, to this palatial structure; and, with the uncontrolled freedom of the boat, spacious dining-room, elegant state-rooms and smoking-room, with abundant opportunity for promenade inside or out, none can fail to enjoy the sail. A cool place can *always* be found in the hottest summer day. This line is particularly desirable for tourists on the morning trains from the South or West. RETURNING, the cars leave Boston at the Providence Depot at 8, P.M., and reach New York at 6, A.M.

TICKETS AND STATE-ROOMS SOLD, AND BAGGAGE checked, in New York, to Boston and all points East; and in Boston, at 82 Washington Street, and Providence Depot, to New York and all points South and West.

The City of Boston. — If we depart from the general plan of this work, to take special note of a great city, it is because Boston stands out in marked distinctiveness from every other city on the continent, — perhaps it should be said, from all others of the whole world. For a certain class of vacation tourists, Boston contains as much to study and enjoy as is found by other classes in the peaceful woods, the mountain sublimities, or the ocean's grand moods. The claim to pre-eminence among all our cities, for lavish profusion and unstinted generosity in all matters pertaining to moral, intellectual, and philanthropic progress, is conceded to Boston, without dispute. Nor are these characteristics spasmodic or ephemeral. From the earliest history of the Puritanical settlements, this distinction has marked the history of Massachusetts, with Boston as the chief and centre of its manifestations. Institutions of learning; of moral and Christian teaching; of broad and comprehensive philanthropy; of art; of æsthetic culture; of hygiene; of all which tends to refine, purify, and elevate the race, — are not merely found here, but are full of progressive vigor. It is the innumerable systems of these classes, which induce many summer tourists to dwell for a season in Boston. We shall not delay to particularize these; for they would require a book to detail them.

For tortuous and narrow streets, lanes, courts, and alleys, no city of equal size can or would compete with Boston. Its plan, if it can be called such, may have been original with wandering cows and sheep; but no other design could ever have devised it as originally built since the late fire, however, many of the streets have been widened and extended, thus bringing some regularity out of seeming chaos; and the general architecture has been greatly improved, and in many cases is rich and elegant. The contrast of costly edifices, side by side with tumble-down ricketiness, is not to be found. What remain, even, of the older buildings are rapidly giving way to new. Widening of streets is progressing at enormous cost; and the demand for business facilities finds ample wealth to meet it. The city proper may be pleasantly studied.

Rare, beautiful, and refreshing to the eye as is Boston Common, the pride of Bostonians, the suburbs are even more attractive and grateful. We doubt if there is a city in the world with such a clustering zone of half city, half-country, — half nature, half art, — as adorns the environs of Boston. The peninsula being so much absorbed by trade, the population is forced to "roost" outside. Here, then, wealth and refined taste are free to combine and adorn. The stranger needs no special directions. Any course will suffice for the start; and the net-work of interlaced steam, horse-car, and carriage roads will permit one to study the whole of the delicious panorama, before finishing the day. Or, taking one of the easy, luxurious carriages with which the city abounds, you may make the sweep first to Chelsea on the north, and, moving always to the left, traverse twenty or thirty miles of constant panorama, filled with beauty and diversity, and finish by a return through Roxbury or South Boston. It is true, every great city has its peculiar and undeniable attractions; but, upon the whole, Boston probably is the one, among them all, that most excels in its suburbs and rural retreats.

Another day, or more, can be spent with equal profit and pleasure in the harbor. The stranger has only to turn to the daily papers for information regarding the many "popular resorts, and how to reach them," to be found in the vicinity of the " Athens of America."

Scarborough Beach, Me., is another of those resorts which still preserve very much of their old-time and old-fashioned freshness; with social quiet, good frolics, plenty of chance for rambling and courting, fishing and shooting. It is quite a favorite resort. Reached by the "Boston and Maine Railroad."

Rye Beach, N.H., half a century ago had an occasional straggling admirer, or, possibly, a company from the back country, in the summer season, to appreciate its beauties and enjoy its lonely solitude. But it has since acquired a distinctive fame. At present its popularity is widely established; and thousands make it their resort for recreation and rest. It is animated and exhilarating in "the season," and is able to maintain its partial preference against all rivals of the coast. It is abundantly supplied with every source of enjoyment, — city, country, sea, and fashionable elegancies and refinements, and all modes and moods of life, to suit all tastes. Visitors must take the "Eastern Railroad."

The Adirondacks of New York have sprung into sudden and universal fame and favoritism. The region has all the novelty of a primeval land, diversified by every variety of landscape and unsearched solitudes; and has the freshness and rare novelty of guides, who alone know the secret wealth of this new Paradise. The atmosphere is remarkably pure, and free from malarious poisons and from chilling damps; so that sudden colds and tormenting fever heats are scarcely known. At present the Adirondacks may boast of its primitive charms; but the region will, doubtless, be materially altered, in this respect, ere long, as visitors to this region are annually numbered by thousands.

Portage, some three hundred and sixty miles from New York City, by the Erie Road, will tempt the tourist to a few days' tarry, and fully repay for the time.

SHELTER ISLAND.

"MANHANSET-AHA-CUSHA-WOMMUCK."

Literally "An Island sheltered by Islands."

A REFERENCE to the map of Long Island will discover near its eastern extremity an inlet known as "Peconic," or Gardiner's Bay. This bay contains a number of beautiful islands, the most prominent of which bears the above appellation. From the days when the red man, in his birch canoe, glided over these beautiful waters; or through the rise and fall of the whale fishery, when Greenport, the principal town, was in the height of its prosperity,— to the present time, Shelter Island, by whatever name it has been called, has always been known as a most charming

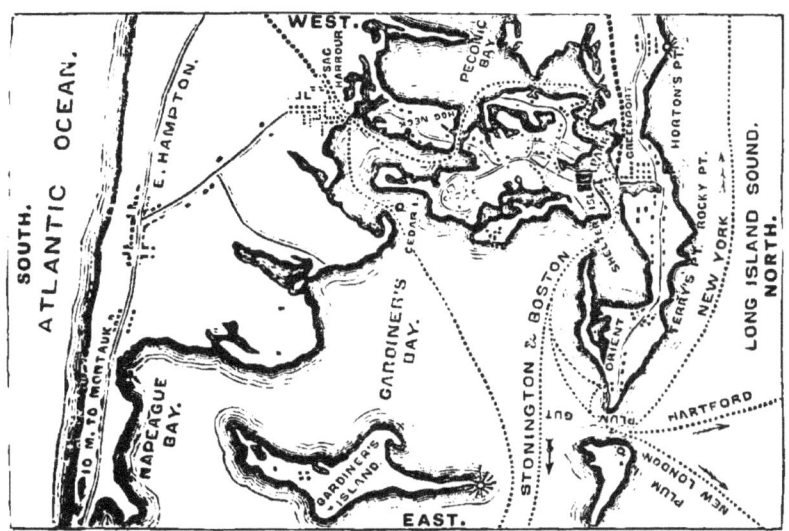

spot. This island contains about nine thousand acres. The surface is undulating; and the soil is rich and productive, while bowlders of great size are found. The red sandstone, from Middletown on the Connecticut River; the gray gneiss, white quartz, sandstone, and variegated granite, from Connecticut, Massachusetts, New Hampshire, and Canada,— are all represented. The remains of primeval forests still exist,— groves of gigantic oak, interspersed with cherry-trees of unusual size, evergreen and locust groves, the latter making the atmosphere redolent with their rich fragrance; while native vines and creepers everywhere abound, and from the forest trees hang in a thousand artistic forms.

SHELTER-ISLAND PARK.

Two hundred acres of the northern portion of the island bear the above appellation. This is adjacent to the village of Greenport, L.I., and is only separated from it by the harbor, at this point less than a mile in width. The surface is varied and undulating, rising in the interior to a height of sixty feet above the water, sloping gently down to the shore on Dering Harbor, and terminating in an abrupt bluff, frequently broken by picturesque ravines, presenting numerous sites for cottages and villas, most of them commanding grand views of land and water scenery.

The sea-front of Locust Point, opposite Greenport, presents a bluff from twenty to fifty feet high, crowned by open groves of locust, oak, hickory, cherry, &c., abounding in grape-vines, Virginia creeper, and other trailing plants. From this a natural ravine leads down to the water, at the mouth of which a fine wharf for a steamboat landing has been constructed.

MANHANSET HOUSE,
Shelter-Island Park.

The location of the Manhanset House is grand and imposing. It rises high above the surrounding country, and from the entrance of the bay, as we sail up the harbor, is the one absorbing object of attraction.

It stands on a bluff fifty feet above the water, and is reached from the wharf by a concrete walk — an inclined plane of easy grade — to steps which lead to the main entrance on the northern front. The walk also continues to the western or carriage entrance; and a branch leads to the eastern entrance. A drive-way follows up the ravine, by which guests who desire are taken to the house.

The main building is two hundred feet long, with an L of two hundred feet; along which are verandas fifteen feet in width, both of which command a view of the boat-landing. The main building fronts the north, securing for its veranda, which commands the harbor from shore to shore, perpetual shade. The house is located to give a water-view from every window. An octagon is constructed in the eastern angle, from which rises a tower to the height of one hundred and seventy-six feet above the water. Into this a stairway leads from the fourth story to look-out rooms on the floors above. These, with the open balconies which entirely surround them, command one of the most magnificent panoramic views imaginable.

From the main entrance a broad passage leads through the house: this is bisected by another running from end to end, each terminating in broad doors, by which the most perfect ventilation is secured. The large public parlor is to the left, with folding-doors opening to the octagon in the base of the tower, which commands a charming view of two hundred and seventy degrees, embracing the steamboat-landing and harbor beyond. From the main entrance the gentlemen's parlor opens to the right, with several private parlors beyond, all fronting the harbor. The office is directly in front, with the main stairway, wash and coat rooms, barber's shop, and other offices, on either side. A long and commodious billiard-hall occupies the basement of the western end, which proves a very attractive feature, particularly in rainy weather.

The main dining-hall, seventy-six feet long, is located in the L, with windows commanding a fine water-view opening to the east. Beyond the dining-hall are the serving-rooms, pantries, kitchen, &c., embracing all modern improvements in the culinary art; while the bakery, chill-room, ice-room, store-rooms, laundry, drying-rooms, and servants' rooms, are in the basement below, which opens to a broad veranda. The boiler-room is located in a separate house contiguous to the main building.

Broad stairways lead to the second story; a walk runs from end to end of the main building and L, affording a fine opportunity to exercise in unpleasant weather. They each terminate in open balconies, which command unrivalled views. The ladies' parlor is directly over the main entrance, with a broad balcony in front. The rooms of the main building are divided into suites, with bath-rooms on the same floor. An open balcony surrounds the octagon, and forms an important feature.

The third story is arranged almost precisely like the second, except the ladies' parlor.

The fourth story is also arranged with desirable rooms, and all modern conveniences. All the stories are high, the rooms large and airy, the passages and verandas broad; and every feature of improvement has been made which would add to the comfort or pleasure of guests.

LOCATION.

The hotel is situated in the midst of a beautiful open grove, which is permeated by drives and walks. The eastern border is covered by a large growth of hickory, maple, cherry, sassafras, chestnut, and oak, some of these original forest trees, to the depth of from sixty to eighty rods. The shore of Haven's Creek is wooded throughout its length. Within this belt of forest is an open area of sixty acres, upon which here and there rise a few wide-spreading oaks and hickories. Shelter-Island Park was laid out by R. Morris Copeland, Esq., landscape gardener, Philadelphia, and presents the attractions of nature beautified by art. It affords sites for villas and cottages in great variety, and is possessed of advantages for summer life rarely found.

SUMMER LIFE.

The coast line of Shelter Island is remarkably tortuous, consisting of points and inlets, which undoubtedly accounts for the abundance of fish everywhere to be found. About two-thirds of the island has been under cultivation. Shelter Island was included in the crown grant to the Earl Stirling, in 1636, and was bestowed by him as a gift to his agent James Farrett. He sold it in 1641 to Stephen Goodyear, Deputy Colonial Governor of Connecticut; and he conveyed it to Capt. Nathaniel Sylvester and his brother Constant Sylvester of Boston, and Thomas Rouse and

Thomas Middleton, merchants of Boston, for "*sixteen hundred pounds of good merchantable muscovado sugar.*" Through an act of confiscation by the Dutch Governor of New York, Anthony Colve, the whole island fell into the possession of Nathaniel Sylvester, and was bequeathed by him in equal shares to his five sons.

STIRLING OAKS.

Among the curiosities of Shelter Island Park is a group of Stirling oaks of original growth, whose wide-spreading branches afford a cool and delightful shade.

It was settled mainly from New England about 1650, and has at present some seven hundred inhabitants. The archives of the older families, now resident upon it, are full of interesting history of the Colonial and Revolutionary periods.

AMUSEMENTS.

The drives which traverse the island in all directions are full of picturesque variety; and the views from some of the higher lands, in extent and beauty, are not exceeded by those of any watering-place south of Mt. Desert. The surface of the roads is fine, the soil being particularly adapted to that purpose.

The prevailing cool south-west breeze, and the dry, balmy atmosphere, give a special charm to this climate.

Dering Harbor affords perfectly land-locked anchorage for yachts in from two to five fathoms; while the surrounding waters of Gardiner's and Peconic Bays, and Shelter Island and Long Island Sound, furnish every variety of excellent sailing. The coast-survey charts are most detailed in their record of soundings, buoys, and light-houses.

Fish abound in great variety, and it is only necessary to add, in quantities so abundant that many persons gain a livelihood by taking them.

The crystal clearness of the water adds to the pleasure of the bathers. The tide rises and falls but three feet, which gives additional security to this healthful amusement.

Sportsmen will be attracted to this locality by the abundance of plover, woodcock, quail on the upland, snipe on the beaches, and ducks, coots, and other water-fowl in the bays which surround Shelter Island.

COMMUNICATIONS.

Few places naturally isolated are so accessible as Shelter Island. The steam-ferry, which plies constantly between Greenport and Shelter-Island Park, virtually connects them. Several trains run daily on the Long Island Railway, which terminates at Greenport. A line of steamers leaves New York at evening, by which guests are landed at Shelter Island on the following morning. Lines of boats run daily between Shelter Island and New London and Saybrook, Conn., connecting directly with the "Shore Line" and "Connecticut Valley" Railroads, and through them with the entire railroad system of New England.

For further information, address *Manhanset House, Shelter-Island Park, New York.*

FRED. H. GOULD, *Proprietor.*

Saratoga Springs, N.Y. — Elsewhere, very brief allusion is made to Saratoga and to Niagara Falls. These famous places are so well known and generally understood, that any special account of their peculiarities would seem to be unnecessary and superfluous. Possibly, however, more particular notice may be desirable by some who read this work, to aid in deciding " Where am I to go? " in vacation time, and who wish to consider the whole field. Saratoga Springs may be visited from New York City, either by the Hudson River to Albany, or by the New York Central Railroad; and a new and very desirable route, from the romantic scenery it passes, is *via* Central Railroad of New Jersey, through Mauch Chunk, Wilkesbarre, Scranton, &c. (see description of Central Railroad of New Jersey); or from Boston, — circuitous but diversified and charming routes, — by various railroads; those from the Fitchburg, the Boston and Albany, and the Lowell passing through every description of inhabited, rural, and mountainous regions, and therefore to be preferred. Taking either of these initial points as the starting-place, ample novelties will invite one's leisure throughout the distances travelled. The chief places of special interest found by the New York line of travel have already been noted. The sweep around the country required by the Boston start is rich in natural and artificial wonders. Commencing at either of the named Boston stations, the first hour passes in the midst of delightful towns and villages, which are mere tributaries of Boston, and are sustained by, and aid to sustain, the great "Hub." Here are residences of perfect taste, and surrounded by rural charms, filling the minds of visitors with continued pleasure. Some of the places through which the lines of travel pass are renowned in Colonial and Revolutionary histories. Those routes which converge at Fitchburg diverge again towards Saratoga Springs, Niagara Falls, the Adirondacks, Lake George, the White Mountains of New Hampshire, and the healthful quietudes of the Green Mountains of Vermont. Whichever course is preferred, the enthusiasm of the refined traveller constantly warms and renews as the glory and splendor of summer verdure, of hills, valleys, meadows, purling streams, and cosey homes, — all speeding by like the flight of birds, — break upon the vision in ever-varying novelty and freshness. It may well be remarked here, that no veteran of the road ever prepares for a pleasure jaunt without first procuring tables of railroad and water lines of communication, and thoroughly mastering his course of march and how he will proceed. He then secures his through ticket, and is prepared to enjoy his pleasure campaign, without the flutter and annoyance of constant doubt as to whither he is moving, and where any change of base should be made. Ladies, especially, ought to ponder this hint.

Should your course from Boston be towards Niagara Falls or the Adirondacks or Quebec, your departure is made from Fitchburg by a different line from the one to be chosen if the aim be for the mountain regions of New Hampshire or Vermont. This the intelligent reader will readily understand. Of course, should you curve around towards the populous State of New York, the chief features of the country will be studded by characteristics of man's busy industry and aggregation into communities. But in the sparsely settled States of New Hampshire and Vermont, Nature still reigns in undisturbed stillness, and in the full beauty and bloom of her pristine charms.

Having decided, then, by what ways you will approach, say, Saratoga Springs, and having reached that fashionable Mecca at last, what are you to do? What is is there to be "done"? Simply nothing, or nearly that, except to drink water from one or all of the thirty odd medicinal springs of the place, and be fashionable, according to the sickly sentimentality of that health restoring and destroying spot.

"Like Newport by the sea, Saratoga is often called the Queen of American watering-places; and this dual sovereignty is generally acknowledged. The hotel system of Saratoga is unrivalled elsewhere in the world; and, although equal to the accommodation of eighteen thousand guests, it is taxed to its utmost capacity in the month of August (the season opens early in June). Broadway is the main street, and extends for several miles, with the chief hotels near its centre, and a succession of costly villas beyond. The village is at its brightest in August, when it is thronged with visitors, and thousands of private and public carriages join in the parade of fashion on Broadway and the boulevard. During the 'height of the season,' the crowds to be seen in all public places, the brilliant balls at the grand hotels, the music of excellent bands, and the many other excitements always prevailing,—make up a scene probably unequalled in the world."

The whole sum of natural scenery, worthy of a walk or ride, afforded by the Saratoga Springs area, is surpassed by almost any rural resort of our land. If the springs were to dry up, the birds of fashionable plumage would flit forever, and the whole of that now populous and prosperous resort would "dry up" as well.

While approaching Saratoga, and within an easy radius of that place, the lover of old stories and romantic adventures may find abundant food for contemplation in hunting up the many historic fields of wilderness campaigns, renowned in the quaint old primitive days. Encounters between our Colonial ancestors and the French and Indians,—extending from Canada, over wilderness and lake, on to Saratoga itself,—with their startling and bloody incidents, fill the mind with a strange fascination. Every schoolboy knows the story, especially the last scene, when the boastful Burgoyne surrendered to the sturdy patriots under Gates, in

Revolutionary times. Those whose tastes incline to the study of battle-fields will find ample attractions within convenient reach from Saratoga.

Having worked up the great springs, and toned up by them possibly, the trip is continued into the Adirondacks, or to romantic Lake George, or Niagara Falls and to Quebec, at pleasure. The Adirondacks may be approached from several directions of travel, — the lines towards the springs and the famous mountain region "forking" at Rutland, Vt. In either case, however, Lake Champlain is the point, if it can be called a "point," to be reached; and now taking steam-travel to Plattsburg, places one on the proper spot to commence investigations of the Adirondacks.

The scenery by rail and steamer, from Saratoga Springs to Lake George, thence on to Lake Champlain and the Adirondacks, is not surpassed, for novelty, beauty, or grandeur, by any known resorts for strangers and guests in the world. To become even tolerably familiar with the leading and more striking features of that vast panorama would require many seasons and assiduous study.

Starting from Saratoga, — or by any of the numerous routes which converge at **Niagara Falls**, — the traveller or wonder-hunter finds himself at last in the presence of that world-renowned glory of the waters. Description of those stupendous Falls has been exhausted long ago. No attempt at details will be made here. There are other sublimities of nature, no less equal in their impressiveness and startling grandeur. There are water leaps of loftier heights, and amid scenes that fill the soul with delight and awe. But no such vast volume, no like rush and turmoil and thunder, has yet been discovered in the habitable parts of the globe. We find inexpressible delight and profound emotion in every variety of earth's peculiar, more exceptional, and fanciful aspects, — in the tender and sweet calm of woodland green, and shady solitudes of rills and wild flowers and birds, and the wavy mists of remoter hills; in the great stabs and scars which mighty convulsions have inflicted; in the stern and sterile summits where ice and snow forever reign; in the cascades, the sinuous streams, the wave-washed crags of the Atlantic shores. But from none of these come such profound impressions as from the awful plunges and the reverberating thunders of Niagara Falls. With a thousand pretentious rivals, it is the crowned monarch of them all.

To **Quebec**, from the Falls, — first to Lewiston, then by boat upon Lake Ontario, and thus to Toronto, thence to Kingston, and so on to Montreal, and finally to Quebec, — will prove as fascinating a tour, in its innumerable and singularly wild and beautiful "sights," as heart could desire.

Many make this a special and final trip, dwelling leisurely at various interesting localities, and then turning homeward. Great numbers, however, make the full circle, — taking in the Springs, Watkins Glen (see description), the Falls, the Lakes, the turbulent St. Lawrence, the towns and cities; through to Montreal; and then by the more northerly course to the Green and the White Mountains; and finally the lake resorts in New Hampshire; and back through the manufacturing industries and sea-side charms of Massachusetts. The northern portions of the country thus afford an almost bewildering record of places, of every diversified class, for summer seekers after pleasure, rest, and recuperated health

In this work will be found the amplest suggestions for the consideration of all; but we will venture to advise the weak and more feeble, seeking appetite and strength, to make the tour first by the Springs, the Glen, and the Falls, to Quebec; and then into Vermont, on to New Hampshire, and close at the sea-shore of Massachusetts; not overtasking the love of nature or art by any fatiguing efforts; not to haste too much, nor dwell long in any one place; but move on at perfect leisure, yet with sufficient speed to keep the mind constantly in a gently pleased state.

In a majority of cases it will be found, that, on reaching the hilly regions and the pure air (the lung-food) of Vermont and New Hampshire, there comes a sense of improved strength; more elasticity and decision of mind; a call from the stomach for food, which begins to be relished with unwonted craving, and even Johnny-cakes " taste good."

Pills and tonics and bitters, and "coddling" a reluctant stomach, are doctor's remedies, furnished for fees. But Nature's pharmacy is the only safe and sure resort for renewing one's health.

Clifton Springs " are in Ontario County, New York, near **Seneca Lake,** and on the route by way of Watkins Glen. (See Northern Central Railroad.) The surrounding country, in all directions, is particularly interesting; and many remarkable points are within accessible distance. The waters are scientifically described as being calcic-sulphur, and are recommended as highly beneficial in certain diseases. They were first utilized in 1806 by the erection of suitable buildings for the accommodation of those who resorted to them from the surrounding country. Since then great improvements have been made; and the Springs now enjoy a wide popularity."

Star Island, N.H., is the queen resort of the *Isle of Shoals*, "cradled in sea," ten miles off the coast. It is unrivalled for its fine fishing, and for its cool, invigorating atmosphere. The stanch little steam yacht "Major" with accommodations for 150 passengers, connects with the Eastern Railroad at Portsmouth. Tourists can leave Boston at 8, A.M., and return at 4, P.M.

Engraved expressly for "Bachelor's Popular Resorts, and How to Reach Them."

SUMMER LIFE AT NORTH MOUNTAIN HOUSE

THE NORTH MOUNTAIN HOUSE.

One of the most important problems to determine in household matters is, "Where shall we spend the hot months of summer?" A change is required; we must go somewhere. The father has become overtaxed by the cares of business; the mother is wearied by household duties; the children need a respite; the health of all demands this change. "But where can we go?" are the oft-repeated words.

Why, there are places enough, — by the sea, at the springs, or in the mountains. The newspapers teem with notices of them; and books resound with their praises. At Cape May, Atlantic City, Long Branch, or Newport; at Bedford Springs, Saratoga, Watkins Glen, or Niagara; at the White Mountains, Mount Desert, Mauch Chunk, or Cresson; and at hundreds of other fashionable resorts, — houses in abundance are open, servants are ready, and landlords stand smiling at the door to receive you. Their halls dazzle with beauty; their parlors rustle with fashion; their corridors resound with mirth; and their drives are a whirl of excitement. Certainly, with such an array, one need not lack for a choice.

But it is just this rustle of fashion, this whirl of excitement, that deters many of our best citizens from seeking that recreation which their health requires. It was to meet this emergency that the North Mountain House was erected, and a summer home provided where muslin and chintz, common sense and comfort, should supplant the prevailing customs of popular resorts; in a word, where *dress* is not paramount to good taste and social enjoyments. Here are good accommodations for two hundred guests, all amply supplied with the substantial provisions of home, in a climate fresh with invigorating atmosphere, with springs of pure mountain water, where at reasonable rates a man may take his family for the season, and return invigorated and refreshed.

If the reader would locate the North Mountain House, he is referred to that spot on the map of Pennsylvania, between the East and West Branches of the Susquehanna River, where the counties of Sullivan, Luzerne, and Wyoming corner, from which flow the head-waters of Loyal Sock, Muncy, Fishing, Huntington, Kitchen, Bowman, and Mehoopany Creeks. There it stands, on the banks of a charming lake, on the summit of North Mountain, of the Alleghany range, 2,700 feet above tidewater (the highest habitable spot in Pennsylvania), in the centre of an unbroken primeval forest of 25,000 acres, not a house within a half-dozen miles, and "no one to molest or make afraid." The North Mountain House, as a popular resort, is a success. No "rustle of fashion in the parlors;" though its "corridors resound with mirth," and the halls and grounds are radiant with that beauty and alive with that enjoyment which come from good cheer.

There is fishing for those who like it, and hunting in the woods; there is sailing on the lake, and roaming in the groves; there are billiards for rainy days, and croquet for fine; there are scenes for the artist's pencil, and abundant sports for all.

WILD WOODS.

North Mountain is eighteen miles from Shickshinny, on the East Branch of the Susquehanna, through which passes the "Lackawanna and

Bloomsburg" Railroad, connecting north with the "Delaware, Lackawanna and Western," and south with the "Philadelphia and Erie road."

The morning train from Wilkes Barre leaves you at Shickshinny about nine o'clock. A good team can be secured at the hotel; and the drive to North Mountain is delightful. The route is over an excellent upland road, and commands a succession of grand and varied landscape views, in admiration for which the miles grow short, and the distance is the least objectionable feature of the journey. Should necessity require, the trip can be made from the afternoon train; but it is not as pleasant, as we have the evening sun in our eyes, and arrive after nightfall. The road winds among the hills, rising by easy grade to the base of the mountain proper, by which much of its altitude is overcome. The side is steep; but the carriage-way is shaded by forest trees, and is exceedingly picturesque. It is overhung in places by frowning rocks; and the rush of an impetuous stream can be heard in the valley below.

The topography of North Mountain is so different from our general acceptation of the term "mountain,"—which usually rises to a summit crest,—that a brief description of its physical characteristics will be in place. Its sides are abrupt, presenting many interesting geological features. The summit surface is generally level, beneath which the outcropping strata of the carboniferous and sub-carboniferous formations are distinctly visible. This forms an extended plateau, broken by gentle undulations, extending thirty miles in length by ten in breadth. It is covered by a dense forest of primeval trees,—oak, hickory, maple, birch, cherry, hemlock, pine, beech, and other varieties usually grown in much higher latitudes. Springs of pure water, crystal streams alive with speckled trout, and quiet lakelets, abound. On the banks of the largest, *Highland Lake*, the North Mountain House has been erected. This delightful sheet of water, three miles in circumference, is fed by springs at its bottom. It abounds in fine varieties of fish, and furnishes withal a pleasing source of amusement. Its outlet forms the head-waters of *Kitchen Creek*, which, with seeming reluctance at first, leaves its parent head; then, as it moves along, gathering strength by fresh accessions, it soon assumes a bolder course, until the mountain's brink is reached, down which it plunges impetuously, forming numerous wild cascades, then, with a fearful leap sheer down the deep abyss, is dashed into snowy spray among the rocks. Rich, luxuriant foliage depends from the overhanging cliffs, through which peers the sparkling sheen of a midsummer's day, clothing all in bright rainbow hues.

"**Ganoga Falls**" are 127 feet high. They are of recent discovery, and must prove a great acquisition to the attractions of North Mountain. They are three miles from the house, by a picturesque woodland road.

Engraved expressly for "Bachelder's Popular Resorts, and How to Reach Them."
GANOGA FALLS NORTH MOUNTAIN PA

The immediate approach is wild in the extreme, affording an opportunity at comparatively small effort to witness Nature clothed in her native dress.

MOUNTAIN STREAM.

The stream continues down the mountain side, forming a series of wild cataracts and charming cascades, and is also a delightful resort for the angler.

The enduring character of the conglomerate and hard sandstone formation protects the surface to the mountain's brink; but the deep gorges through which the maddened streams have cut their way, exposing the formation from surface to base, furnish a field for the geologist, of unusual interest, and to the student and lover of wild and romantic scenery scenes worthy of the artist's pencil.

NORTH MOUNTAIN VIEW.

The "North Mountain View" is one of the most remarkable features of this character. It is on the south-west side of the mountain, less than a half-mile from the house, and is of easy access. To the spectator from the head of this wild and broken cañon, the scene is indescribable by the artist's pencil or writer's pen. It is a singular combination of scenery, possessing the grandest features, clothed with the picturesque and beautiful, over and beyond which — stretching far, far away — is that immeasurable distance which always "lends enchantment to the view."

A visitor writing of it says, "Here, standing on a perpendicular ledge of rocks, you gaze with a mixture of wonder and admiration down upon this magnificent view. Seven distinct mountain ranges dovetail one into the other, forming a long, deep gorge, through which you look for miles beyond miles. . . . Far into the unseen depths of the ravine below is heard the roaring of a creek, of which occasional glimpses are seen sparkling in the noonday sun." The accompanying cut is from an original sketch by the artist, Thomas Hill; and yet the almost magic touch of that celebrated artist fell far short of the sublime grandeur of nature.

There are those who delight to sail on the lake, to fish in its waters, and walk on its banks; there are those who find pleasure in roaming through the groves and penetrating to the unbroken depths of the forest; there are those who, following the sportive streams from crest to base, watch their falling waters, and amid wreaths of snow-white spray linger for hours to tempt the speckled trout; and those who enter joyously into all the sportive games in which the place abounds. But to none is the delight so sparkling, the pleasure so pure, the joy so lasting, as to the devotee who worships at the shrine of the North Mountain "View." It is *the* great feature of the place, and the walk to it is delightful.

The professional hunter and amateur sportsman will be alike interested in this field for the exercise of their favorite amusements. The North Mountain House consists of two buildings, surrounded and connected by long, broad verandas. The older or stone house was built many years ago, before the days of railroads, on the old turnpike leading from Buffalo, N.Y., to Sunbury, Penn., which is still used by drovers in transporting their stock; and the house is the comfortable home where the weary traveller is sure of a cheerful welcome. Its complete isolation, surrounded by many miles of unbounded forest filled with deer and other large game, soon made it the *rendezvous*, in the autumn and winter months, of hunters and sportsmen. During a day spent there by the writer, in November, 1873, there were four deer and a bear killed in the immediate vicinity, — not an unusual circumstance in the hunting season. The laws of the State protect deer during the summer months; but the autumn finds this a rich field for sport.

Wild fowl, in their migratory flight, frequently make "Highland Lake" their resting-place. Others rear their young in its quiet coves.

FOREST LIFE.

The North Mountain House embraces among its patrons many of the best families of the State, who select for a summer home this healthful locality, convenient of access, yet far away from the false life of *fashionable* resorts; a spot abounding in the pristine beauties of nature. Here they spend the heated term, and return to their homes in autumn recuperated in strength, with fresh vigor to enter again the battle of life.

"**The Virginia Springs.** — Throughout the States of Virginia and West Virginia are distributed a large number of mineral springs, all more or less noted for their medicinal properties, and the beauty of their surroundings. Situated, as they generally are, high up amid the Alleghany ranges, they enjoy the perfection of mountain atmosphere, and an abundance of forest shade. Among these 'fountains of health' may be enumerated the **Augusta Springs,** in Augusta County, Virginia, consisting of both alum and chalybeate waters; **Bath Alum Springs,** in Bath County, Virginia; the **Berkley Springs,** in Morgan County, West Virginia; the **Capon Springs,** in Hampshire County, West Virginia; the **Healing Springs,** in Bath County, Virginia, whose waters correspond very nearly in temperature to the Schlangenbad of Nassau, being from 80° to 84° Fahr., and are recommended as of the highest value in all ulcerous diseases; the **Hot Springs,** in Bath County, Virginia, the temperature of which range, at about 100° Fahr., and are similar in remedial properties to those of the Healing Springs; **Jordan's Rock Alum Springs,** in Frederick County, Virginia; the **Montgomery White Sulphur Springs,** in Montgomery County, Virginia; the **Rawley Springs,** in Rockingham County, Virginia, the waters of which are pronounced the best pure chalybeate in the State; the **Rockbridge Alum Springs,** in Rockbridge County, Virginia; the **Rockbridge Baths,** in Rockbridge County, Virginia; the **Sweet Springs,** in Monroe County, West Virginia; the **Warm Springs,** in Bath County, Virginia, similar in character to the Hot and the Healing Springs, and of about the same temperature; the **Yellow Sulphur Springs,** in Montgomery County, Virginia; and the **Greenbrier White Sulphur Springs,** in Greenbrier County, West Virginia. These last-named springs are among the best known in the United States, and, according to a late medical writer, very much resemble the celebrated cold sulphur waters of Nenndorf, in Electoral Hesse. They are beneficial in a wide range of diseases, embracing those of the liver, the skin, and others of a similar character. These springs are the Mecca of all Virginia tourists, the resort of the gay and fashionable, a place where pleasure-seeking reigns supreme. They are located in a beautiful valley, near the summit of the Greenbrier Mountains, about two thousand feet above the sea. Within this valley, overlooked by mountain summits, is the magnificent hotel. In front the broad lawn spreads out, intersected by numerous winding walks. Encompassing the lawn on either side are long lines of shining white cottages, embowered beneath the shade of ancient oaks; while, at the distant extremity, the famous spring bubbles beneath a pavilion. Taking one of the by-paths to the right, the 'Lover's Maze' is soon reached; where obscurely-winding paths lead in every direction amid a thick growth of laurel; here the 'season' throws a spell of animation and revelry."

Gloucester, Mass., is the great centre of the New England fishing interests. Thousands of her hardy population pursue their perilous avocation at all seasons of the year, and upon all the great fishing-grounds, especially upon the Banks of Newfoundland. No season passes without its sad tragedies among the vast fleet which leaves the harbor of Gloucester. The sources of pleasure and of cultivated intercourse located around Gloucester are worthy of an elaborate detail, and are full of agreeable surprises and rare delights. Great numbers take the cars of the "Eastern Railroad," or boats from Boston direct, in the travelling season.

Rockport, Mass., was once a part of Gloucester. This place will not attract a great deal of attention from sight-hunters, although its extensive granite-quarries will richly repay a visit.

The famous and justly popular resort called **Pigeon Cove** is close by Rockport. This and other spots of novel and rare curiosities form a group of too much interest to be overlooked; and it has long been a fixed centre for a very large summer attendance. Few places on the New England coast afford greater gratifications to visitors. The trip is made by the "Eastern Railroad."

Moosehead Lake, Me. This popular summer resort was formerly visited exclusively by fishing and hunting parties, but is fast becoming known to the summer tourists, and sought for by families and individuals seeking rest or recreation. Here the pleasure hunter will find wild scenery, — rocks and woodland; water views, with good lake and brook fishing; and dense forests, with plenty of game. Reached from Boston by the Eastern or Boston and Maine Railroads, and the Maine Central to Dexter, Me., thence thirty miles by stage to Greenville, and steamer to Mount Kenio. Shortest time twenty-two hours from Boston.

Falls of Montmorenci, and **Saguenay River.** — While at Quebec the tourist should not fail to visit the Falls of Montmorenci and the Saguenay River. The former are nine miles below the city, and have a leap of two hundred and fifty feet. The "Saguenay" is reached by steamer, also by the Grand Trunk Railway. This river embodies some of the grandest scenery on the continent. It is filled with chasms, cascades, and rapids. The solid walls of rock which hem it in rise perpendicularly hundreds of feet, and in many places present a surface apparently finished by the hand of man. The adjacent region is made up of rare and interesting scenery, at present little known to the traveler.

EXCURSION TO OAK BLUFFS AND KATAMA BAY.

THE coast of New England abounds in beautiful harbors, charming bays, and quiet inlets, many of which are unknown to the public for want of means of communication. But the popular and increasing custom of spending the summer months at the sea-shore every year causes the development of new and delightful resorts, — localities whose quiet beauty frequently proves a surprise to the travelling public. Yet it has so often happened that a long time intervenes before such accommodations are prepared, that tourists have hesitation in visiting any but the beaten tracks of travel. Very fortunately, however, this difficulty is being largely obviated by the action of business men, who, with a quick eye for the beautiful, and sharp discernment for the wants of the public, do not hesitate, on discovering a desirable locality, to announce it with

STEAMBOAT "MARTHA'S VINEYARD" PASSING OAK BLUFFS.

hotel accommodations complete. Such is the case at KATAMA BAY, where the first building erected was a large and commodious hotel. The name of "Katama" is not a familiar one; and many will read it now for the first time. If such, however, will look at the map of Massachusetts, they will see off the eastern shore of Martha's Vineyard a bay or channel separating it from Chappaquiddick Island, which forms the point. This beautiful sheet of water is but eight miles south-east from Oak Bluffs, now so extensively known as a summer resort, and has for the past few years been an objective point for guests from that place.

Tourists by rail to New Bedford connect with the fine side-wheel boats "Martha's Vineyard" and "Monohansett," of the Martha's Vineyard Line of steamers, for Oak Bluffs and Katama.

The excursion from New Bedford is one of the pleasantest on the coast. We have a fine view of Fairhaven as we sail down the harbor. This town is pleasantly located; and a number of beautiful private residences, half hidden by foliage, overlook the water. An old fort stands upon a rocky promontory at the east entrance of the harbor, opposite to which, upon an island, is the light-house. At this point we enter Buzzard's Bay, and cross directly to "Woods Hole," a dozen miles away.

Buzzard's Bay and Vineyard Sound are so protected by headlands and outlying islands, that the sail is delightful. While the coast turns back to the left, after passing the fort, on the right the main-land pushes out into the sea, forming a cape, on which Clark's Point Light-house stands, and Fort Tabor occupies a commanding position. From this the bay opens to the right; and the main-land stretches away in the distance to a marked promontory known as "Round Hill." "Dumpling" or Round Hill Light stands on an isolated rock off this point, beyond which is the main entrance to Buzzard's Bay. The Elizabeth Islands are on the opposite side of the channel. These are individually known by their Indian names, commencing with the westernmost, as Cuttyhunk, Pennikeese, Neshawana, Peskeneese, Naushon, Nonnamensett, and to complete the rhyme, mariners have added, Woods Hole, Quequonkesset. Turning to the left, the main-land, extending towards Cape Cod, can be seen in the blue distance, with Black Rock, a dangerous shoal, lying between. As we approach Woods Hole, the island of Naushon stretches six or seven miles away to our right. This is the property of Capt. John M. Forbes of Boston. His summer residence, and that of his son, form conspicuous features in the landscape. An extensive grove of beech and oak has been stocked with deer, where his friends are annually entertained with a genuine deer-hunt.

The entrance to Woods Hole is narrow and tortuous, with sunken rocks on either side, requiring great nautical skill in its passage. The harbor is small, but deep, and well protected. A hundred houses, perched upon the surrounding hills, many of them quite beautiful, comprise the town; the depot of the Old Colony Railroad being the most conspicuous feature. Visitors to Katama or Oak Bluffs who prefer to go to this place by rail can take the cars at the Old Colony Depot, Boston, and continue from here by boat. The light-house, with its beacon light, stands on a headland at the mouth of the harbor, and marks the entrance to Vineyard Sound. The sail across the sound is delightful. Martha's Vineyard lies directly before you. Gay Head Light is seen far away to the right, while Falmouth Heights are on the left.

VINEYARD HAVEN.

This town, formerly called Holmes' Hole, is approached between two headlands, known as the "East" and "West Chop." Its harbor is indeed a haven for the storm-driven mariner; and hundreds of sail frequently lay here for days awaiting a favorable wind. The village of Vineyard Haven rests upon a hillside, sloping gently to the water.

The town is old; several churches, a few newly erected residences, and an old wind-mill whose arms point to the past, form the conspicuous features in the landscape. By the formation of a natural dike across the southern portion of the harbor, a small lake, three miles long, has been separated from it, known as Lagoon Pond, which is noted

RIDING OUT THE STORM.

for its fine oysters of artificial culture. A carriage-drive along this dike extends, *via* Oak Bluffs, to Katama.

As we leave Vineyard Haven, and the steamer rounds the "East Chop," we approach the locality of summer life for citizens from our large towns. Cottages and villas are scattered over the hillsides, which increase in number and beauty until we reach Oak Bluffs, where we have a *rural* city spread out before us, from which, standing in bold relief, rises a colossal structure surrounded by broad verandas, and surmounted by towering cupolas, — THE SEA VIEW HOUSE, — with the steamboat-landing directly in front.

THE "Sea View" is the prominent feature of the town, which lies beyond. On either side, overlooking the water, and extending for thousands of feet, is a broad plank promenade, with seats the entire length.

At the right is a building one thousand feet long by eighteen feet wide, built into the bluff, protected by a heavy bulkhead. This is used for amusements. The side is of glass, and opens to the sea. In front is a broad promenade, provided with seats. The roof is flat, covered with concrete, and is also used for a walk, over which pavilions are placed at intervals, the whole overlooked by beautiful cottages. At the left of the hotel are hundreds of bathing-houses, with pavilions and seats for spectators. Steamboats and yachts crowd the landing, while the wharves, the verandas, the balconies and bluffs, are filled with the life and gayety of the scene. Over fifty-nine thousand guests visited this renowned resort during the season of 1872.

SEA VIEW HOUSE.
Oak Bluffs, Martha's Vineyard.

If the boat remains at the landing long enough to allow it, a visit to the "Sea View" will amply repay the trouble. From the wharf, the entrance is made through an ornamental gate-house, which is devoted to offices. In the tower at the right is the baggage-room, with a general railway ticket-office over it. At the left is the wharfinger's office, over which is the office of the Oak Bluffs Company. The basement of the hotel is approached by a private entrance from the wharf, by which the baggage and stores are taken, and, by the steam elevator, raised to any part of the house.

Wide passage-ways extend through the basement, cutting each other at right angles. At the left of the entrance, opening to the sea, are the barber's shop, bath-rooms, and billiard-hall, beyond which is the engineer's and boiler room, &c. On the right are store-rooms, ice-house, chill-room, laundry, bakery, and servants' rooms. The house and promenades are lighted by Walworth's solar gas generator, with gas manufactured in an underground building, distant from the hotel.

The Sea View House is approached by a broad flight of steps, leading to a capacious veranda at the east end, twenty-six feet in width. This is an important architectural feature of the house. It is three stories high, giving beauty to the structure, and comfort and pleasure to the guests. It commands a full view of Vineyard Sound, the great "highway of commerce." Ninety-five thousand vessels are reported to have passed Gay Head Light in 1872. The ladies' reception-room is at the right of the entrance, with hat and coat and wash rooms, and stairway beyond. On the left is the gentlemen's reception-room, elevator, and office. Opposite the main entrance, the doors open to the dining-hall, which occupies the entire width of the building, with long windows opening to wide verandas on either side. The private dining-rooms are beyond. Broad stairways and the elevator lead to the stories above.

The public parlor, on the second floor, is pleasantly located across the southern end of the building, commanding, from its windows and balconies, an extended view in three directions. On either side of the passage are private parlors and sleeping-rooms; and the two stories above are similarly arranged, with walks the entire length, affording excellent ventilation. Balconies lead from every story. A tank of two thousand gallons capacity, placed under the roof, supplies the water for the house.

The peak of the south tower has three fine sleeping-rooms. The north tower has two, with a passage-way leading to the lookout-room above, from the four windows of which a most extensive marine and landscape view can be had.

The chapel is a beautiful structure, of ornamental design, and seats eight hundred and twenty-two persons. It stands on a rounded knoll, surrounded by a grove of oak. It is octagonal in form, with four doors, leading from opposite angles, and a gallery entrance on the side, in front of which stands the pulpit, with ante-rooms on either side. The seats on the floor and in the gallery occupy seven sections of an octagon, facing to a common centre. The inside is not plastered; but the painted tri-colored walls and ceiling, relieved by the ornamented framework, produce a singular and beautiful effect. The building is not confined to any particular denomination; but any stockholder can secure the pulpit for a friend on any unengaged day.

The free and harmonious use of a building so beautiful lends a charm to the exercises, and, furnishing as it does a regular place of worship, contributes largely to the popularity of the place.

Circuit Avenue commences at the wharf, and extends through and around the town. It has a paved drive-way, with concrete sidewalks. Other important streets are paved with concrete. The town is emphatically a *Cottage City*. Within an area of one mile stand six hundred and ninety-one cottages. Among the hundreds of beautiful houses, of exquisite architecture, scarcely two can be found alike.

SEASIDE COTTAGE OF HON. E. P. CARPENTER.

Oak Bluffs is a delightful place, frequented by persons of culture and taste, which can only be partially described in this article, but will well repay a visit from the pleasure-seeker. Katama, on the eastern point of the island, is now attracting attention.

The scenery at Katama was so beautiful, the fishing and shooting so unusually fine, that in 1872 a few gentlemen of means determined to erect a hotel there, and secure a building site for others who, like themselves, should be desirous of leaving the heated streets of a town for a quiet cottage life by the seaside. The result was beyond the expectations of the most sanguine; and forty-three persons came forward the first season, and secured lots, with the agreement to build cottages on them. The place has been artistically surveyed by a landscape-gardener, streets and avenues graded, and parks laid out. Summer residences are being built; and a town is springing up as if by magic.

Several of the managers of this enterprise are the same who made Oak Bluffs a success; the same whose lots, placed in the market five years ago at $100 each, have since sold for $1,600; the same who, in six years, from a single house, have built "THE COTTAGE CITY OF AMERICA," with paved and gas-lit streets, — in a word, a complete town, clothed with taste, comfort, and picturesque beauty. And now the same energy and perseverance which succeeded at Oak Bluffs promise success at Katama.

It is a short but pleasant sail across the bay from Oak Bluffs to the village of Edgartown, the spires of which can be seen in the south-east. This place was once a town of some enterprise; but, with the decline of the whale fishery, the young men have generally sought employment elsewhere. From Edgartown we enter Katama Bay, a beautiful sheet of water, some five miles long. It is of itself an excellent harbor, affording not only good anchorage, but is well protected from the winds, making it a favorable resort for yachting and fishing clubs. On entering the bay, "**Mattakeset Lodge**," the model hotel of Katama, becomes the absorbing object of attention.

MATTAKESET LODGE.
Katama, Martha's Vineyard.

The house stands on a commanding bluff, at the opposite end of the harbor, its symmetrical towers cutting boldly against the southern sky. As you near the landing, immediately below the hotel, its peculiar structure and singular location become apparent. The surface at Katama is an extended table-land, broken by gentle undulations, but at the coast falling abruptly to the beach below. In a single instance, by some natural agency, a pathway has been grooved through the bluff to the water's edge, forming an admirable passage, of easy grade, from the beach to the plain above. Here a wharf has been built; and on the bluff, spanning the ravine, stands the hotel, under which the drive-way passes to the town beyond.

"Mattakeset Lodge" has been constructed to afford the *maximum* amount of comfort and pleasure. Numerous balconies and broad verandas, commanding a complete view of the landing and harbor beyond, surround the house; but the peculiar and favorite feature is an open gallery, which occupies the entire upper story. In the evening this is brilliantly lighted by gas, and is entirely devoted to promenading and dancing.

YACHTING.

It is, indeed, a novel feature. Here, in the hottest summer's day, a cooling breeze is always felt, and the roar of the breakers on the south side of the island, scarcely a mile away, fills the air. The whitened foam, as the waves dash upon the beaches, which stretch away like a ribbon in the distance, is always an interesting object of contemplation. From this elevation, high above the surrounding water, securely shielded from the sun's scorching rays, hundreds of whitened sail can be seen.

The admirable facilities for yachting, and the abundance of fish and birds in this vicinity, have induced the proprietors to make special arrangements for the convenience of sportsmen; while others, whose taste for these amusements commences after the game has passed the culinary department, will have reason to be equally well pleased. Fishing parties from Oak Bluffs have come to be daily affairs.

Few localities on the coast possess better facilities for fishing than Katama, — deep-sea fishing off Cape Pogue for cod, haddock, hake, whiting, pollock, and halibut; exciting sport in sailing or trolling for blue fish, striped bass, and Spanish mackerel; still fishing in the bay, within a gun-shot of the house, for scup, tautog, sea-bass, and sea-perch. But the sport in which Katama leads is in the serving of her unrivalled *Clam-bakes*; and, for the convenience of guests, a grand pavilion has been erected for their shelter.

THE MIGHTY CLAM-BAKE.

Tradition gives color to the claim, that the great genius of Mattakeset, the famous and powerful Indian chief of the primitive days, devised the art of preparing the delicious and now world-renowned "CLAM-BAKE." Charles Lamb relates the remarkable way in which "roast pig" was revealed to the "heathen Chinee." Doubtless the claim set up for Mattakeset is quite as authentic as Lamb's bit of tradition; but it is not as full in particulars. Clams of the very finest variety abound in the region around Mattakeset Lodge; and the formula for composing and compounding a clam-bake, in the style of a fine art, is naturally found here. For general satisfaction, we now describe the process: —

First, a huge saucer-like space is dug in the sand or ground, and is well paved over with stones. This may be called the bake-oven. To prepare the grand bake, the "oven" is filled with fuel, intermingled with goodly sized stones. This is fired (the combustible part); and after the stone portions are all thoroughly heated the coals are raked off. The "oven" is now ready. First, a layer of rock-weed is equally spread over the heated surface; next, from fifteen to twenty-five bushels of clams are thrown in, and then covered with another layer of rock-weed; and over that sea-weed is thickly placed. The heat of the oven is sufficient to raise a great cloud of steam from the water of the clams and the weeds; and in about half an hour, the capacious mound of savory bivalves is ready to be borne to the feast-board. Here, drawn butter, salt, pepper, and vinegar, or any of the more pungent relishes of the table, served in convenient dishes, are used to add zest to this notable and popular food. The instruments used to dislodge the clam from the shell, decapitate it, and submit it to the teeth, are simply fingers. Experts at this kind of feed are wonderfully dexterous in the work, and raise huge piles of shells around them in brief time. This is a clam-bake simple. But, to have a compound bake of appetizing temptations most excelling, as frequently served by mine host of "Mattakeset Lodge," lobsters, green corn, fresh fish, chickens, &c., are to be placed among the clams at the outset. With these additions, the rudely improvised feast becomes one not to be surpassed for lusciousness by the skill of a regiment of French cooks. In the opinion of many, the transcendent glory of Mattakeset Lodge lies in its unrivalled clambakes.

COMMUNICATIONS.

Katama possesses admirable facilities for communication by steamers, and the sail is delightful. A new and beautiful steam-yacht, of unrivalled speed, connects with steamers from Woods Hole and New Bedford, at Oak Bluffs; or you can go by rail, a new and elegantly equipped narrow-gauge road having been built from Oak Bluffs to Katama. And the citizens of Edgartown, alive to the requirements of the public, have laid out and constructed a splendid drive-way of twelve miles, extending from Katama to Vineyard Haven, *via* Edgartown and Oak Bluffs. Steamers will run daily. In a word, every thing which experience can dictate is being done to make this a popular summer resort, and a pleasant seaside retreat.

THE SEA-VIEW BOULEVARD.

This fine drive-way, commencing at Katama, extends twelve miles along the coast to Vineyard Haven. It has been constructed by the citizens of Edgartown, to meet the increasing wants of visitors. From Katama to Edgartown it continues along the table-land to and through the village. A couple of miles beyond, it leads down to the sea, approaching it between two smaller bodies of water, which lay contiguous to and parallel with the ocean. That upon the right, and nearer Edgartown, is known as Crystal Lake, — a beautiful pond, one mile in diameter. On the left we pass the foot of San-cha-can-tack-et Lake, which for miles is only separated from the sea on our right by a natural dike, evidently thrown up by some mighty convulsion, or by the action of the waves, beyond the present history of this region. The road-way has been built along this dike, which in places is so narrow that a stone could be tossed into the water on either side. This is a delightful drive; and, although of recent construction, it has attained a great popularity, affording as it does, to persons having objections to boating, the rare opportunity of securing an equally refreshing sea-breeze while riding in a carriage. Nor is this all. Midway between Edgartown and Oak Bluffs the dike has been cut, by the action of the waters, through which, with the tide, the current ebbs and flows.

This channel has been spanned by a bridge four hundred and fifty feet long, affording a rare opportunity for fishing; not merely small, worthless varieties, but blue-fish, bass, flounders, and others of large size, are taken in abundance. This was only needed to secure for ladies and children, or persons averse to boating, the full advantages of the exhilarating sport of fishing, shorn of the disagreeable annoyances of sea-sickness. The Sea-View House, at Oak Bluffs, is but three miles distant, and in full view from the bridge, which is one of its most favorite resorts. Indeed, the Sea-View Boulevard is one of the most enjoyable features of this popular watering-place.

San-cha-can-tack-et Lake is three miles long, and from one to two wide, and is a favorite boating and sailing locality. Cultivated farms rise to a wooded crest on the opposite shores.

The drive from the bridge to Oak Bluffs is along an undulating surface, which will soon undoubtedly be filled with cottages. It affords a fine variety of landscape views, with occasional glimpses of the town beyond, — the Sea-View House always forming the most imposing feature. Island Lake nestles quietly by the wayside, with a miniature island set like an emerald in its centre.

STRANGERS IN BOSTON.

Boston is well supplied with hotels, and, like every city, with cheap and expensive ones; but the Crawford House, which is under the same management as Mattakeset Lodge, will be found one of the most desirable for strangers. It is centrally located, in Scollay's Square, from which point all the city and Metropolitan horse-cars start. It is convenient to all the depots, and is a first-class house in every respect. It is kept on the European plan, with rooms from $1 to $4 per day; and with four dining-halls the proprietor is able to satisfy his guests in style or price. I have no doubt strangers will find this a desirable home while in Boston and vicinity.

THE LAND OF THE PILGRIMS.

THE OLD COLONY RAILROAD.

Who has ever examined the map of Eastern Massachusetts, with its long arm stretching out into the sea,— the land of the "Pilgrim Fathers,"— without feeling a desire to visit it? From Boston to Narragansett Bay, the coast is filled with interesting localities, many of them identified with the early history of the country. The rock-bound shores of Cohasset are noted for their grand marine views; the beautiful harbor of Plymouth is surrounded by localities replete with historic memories; the barren coast of Cape Cod is made interesting by the beautiful summer resorts which line its borders; the sail through **Vineyard Sound**, "the great highway of commerce," to Newport, with Falmouth Heights and the Elizabeth Islands on the right, and Martha's Vineyard, with Oak Bluffs and Gay Head, on the left, is truly delightful. But there is no established coast route by which to visit these localities. Fortunately, however, they can be reached by rail.

The **Old Colony Railroad** leads to them all. Its branches connect all the prominent points of interest with Boston; and its admirable construction and superior equipment render this one of the most popular summer routes.

The original line extended from Boston to Plymouth, Mass., 37½ miles. It now extends to all the principal points in South-Eastern Massachusetts, and to Newport, R.I., embracing about 300 miles of road.

No more beautiful coast-routes can be selected than the line from Boston to Plymouth, through Weymouth, Hingham, Nantasket, Cohasset, Scituate, Marshfield, and Duxbury (the American "station" of the French ocean telegraph), and the route to the Vineyard, skirting the charming shores of Buzzard's Bay.

Notwithstanding this was the earliest settled portion of New England, portions of it still exhibit a primitive wildness. The following are among the noted summer resorts reached by the Old Colony Railroad.

Nantasket Beach is rapidly rising into popularity, although more of a local than a general character. The beach is long, and just like all the sandy frills of our Atlantic coast. The surface is hard, and admirably adapted to driving or bathing. It is but eighteen miles from Boston. Eleven light-houses can be seen from the shore; and it may well be pronounced one of the most delightful watering-places in the country. Sailing and fishing are without limit; and tens of thousands flock to enjoy the varied beauties of the scene, and the soothing temperature of the coast and sea air, daily, when the heated term is in full power.

Cohasset, which was sliced from Hingham, is a glorious spot for all lovers of the moody sea. Here are cliffy rocks enough, with a broken sea-margin, to insure a turbulent ocean even in a comparative calm; and, when old Neptune is in one of his fiery moods, the scenery around the shores of Cohasset rises to a degree of sublimity and grandeur that surpasses description. The wild, picturesque beauties of Cohasset rocks form an admirable subject for the artist's pencil; and here the lover of the beauties of nature delights to linger. **Marshfield**, the home of Webster, will also attract attention. **Duxbury** is thirty-nine miles from Boston. A walk to Captain's Hill, where a monument is being erected to the memory of Miles Standish, forms a pleasant objective point.

Plymouth. — Although the road to Plymouth passes through several thriving and interesting villages, the chief object of the tourist will be a visit to Plymouth itself, — a visit which cannot fail to interest him; and fortunately for his enjoyment, whether his sojourn is for a day or a week, he will find, at the Samoset and Clifford Houses, accommodations which will render his stay agreeable. Plymouth has a world-wide fame. If the orations delivered in honor of "The Pilgrim Fathers" were all printed in one book, it would make a volume fearful to encounter; for those famous "Pilgrims" landed there, as is generally known. Plymouth is a wholesome, steady, well-to-do town, with nothing remarkable about it except its historic notoriety. And yet the pleasure-seeker can find enough here to busy his hands. There is fair shooting at "the Point," some nine miles down the harbor; and sea and pond fishing are abundant. But the harbor is not good for commerce; and the place will depend chiefly upon the direction in which its capital is utilized. At one period Plymouth was of considerable maritime importance. It is but thirty-seven miles from Boston, and is reached in a little more than an hour's ride. The town is well laid out, and pleasantly located, on ground sloping to the water. Burial Hill, above, commands a fine view of the harbor. Pilgrim Hall, with its many curious relics; Plymouth Rock, Cole's Hill, and Clark's Island (where the Pilgrims "rested on Sunday, Dec. 10,

1620," before landing at Plymouth on the 20th), are all interesting places to visit. The vicinity of Plymouth, with its fresh-water lakes and fine drives, also presents objects of interest.

Hingham is really a very pleasant place, and has many agreeable attractions both for the tourist and the temporary resident.

The Cape Cod Division of the Old Colony Railroad extends to Provincetown, the extreme point of Cape Cod, one hundred and twenty miles distant from Boston. The fine harbor at Provincetown presents a refuge

for the storm-driven mariner. The place is inhabited largely by seafaring men; and its thrifty appearance is a fine illustration of what an enterprising community can drag from the sea. It is built on and surrounded by sand-hills; and the earth of its gardens, so green and beautiful, is mostly brought from the mainland. Branches lead from this road, from Cohasset Narrows to Woods Hole, and from Yarmouth to Hyannis, which was the terminus of the road before it was extended to Provincetown.

Hyannis is a pleasant village, and, next to Provincetown, the largest place on the Cape. It is prettily laid out, and ornamented by shade-trees. The inhabitants are engaged in a sea-faring life; and many retired sea-captains and merchants have made this their home. The railroad leads through the village a mile to the sea, where a fine wharf has been constructed. A growing seaside village, a short distance to the west, overlooks the harbor to Vineyard Sound and Martha's Vineyard beyond. A land company has erected a new hotel, for the accommodation of summer guests; and many fine cottages have already been built, and others are in course of construction. The serrated coast from Hyannis to Woods Hole is alternated with fine beaches, summer resorts, and wild lands, where the sportsman and fisherman delight to roam.

The name of "Cape Cod" is synonymous in most minds with sand, sea, and codfish. For the delicate and sensitive devotees of fashion these words have no charm; but, for the more hardy seekers for novelty and pleasure, they indicate shooting, fishing, and pure air. The characteristics of Cape Cod, although having a likeness to the whole coast family of attractions, are, after all, peculiar to itself. It is not an island; and yet it is as really in the arms of the Atlantic as though it were alone in its waters. To be on the shores of "Cape Cod" is to have the alternating humors of the ocean, as much as though it were Nantucket. Of course, Cape Cod is not a town nor a city nor an island; for it is "Cape Cod," and embraces towns, villages, islands, beaches, headlands, rocks, reefs, sand, salt, plover, ducks, coots, and codfish. It is of varied pleasures, found in numerous and peculiar places.

TROUT POND.

There is **Cotuit Port**, for example, nestled on high land, and in a charming location, almost romantic. It is also the rural home of many families of taste. Few summer resorts surpass it. It is reached by the Old Colony Railroad and connecting stages.

Falmouth Heights, a rising place, with rare attractions, now in process of development by a company of capitalists. It is a delightful location, and commands a fine view of Vineyard Sound. The prospect opens to the south; the ground is high, falling gently from a wooded crest to the bluff, which drops thirty feet to the beach below. Serpentine walks and drives permeate the groves of oak, in which cottages are pleasantly placed. A grand ocean avenue leads for miles along bluff and through the groves to the point of starting. A commodious hotel is open to guests in summer. The railroad which leads to Falmouth Heights and Woods Hole branches from the main road at Cohasset Narrows. This locality abounds in fine landscape and marine views; and summer residences will soon dot the scene.

Woods Hole is a picturesque hamlet of a hundred buildings, located on a promontory, on the extreme southern point of the peninsula which forms Barnstable County. The harbor is small, but affords good anchorage, and is well protected by outlying headlands and islands. This is the terminus of the road in this direction, and is the nearest point of railroad connection to Martha's Vineyard, and shorter by one hour than by any other route. To insure connections, the company run a line of steamers from their depot on the wharf to Oak Bluffs, Vineyard Haven, and Katama, — a short and pleasant sail across Vineyard Sound. Connection is also made at Woods Hole with the Nantucket Steamship Company's boats to Oak Bluffs and Nantucket.

Oak Bluffs. — It may well be inferred that a resort supporting so many lines of steamboats is one of more than ordinary popularity. Oak Bluffs, as a summer resort, is a success; and its magical growth has fairly earned for it the appellation of *The Cottage City of America*. A full description of the place will be found elsewhere. Oak Bluffs is also connected, by a narrow-gauge railroad and by a line of steamers, with Katama, — a new resort, with a fine hotel, opened to the public last season.

Nantucket — a word significant of a hardy, brave, honest, and hospitable community — is another of the decayed triumphs of the harpoon and the whale. Located in mid-ocean, its people rarely seen on land, a Nantucketer is a novelty seldom met, unless one goes where he resides. For years this most healthful and agreeable spot was little known, except as "Nantucket," and in no wise sought by the traveller, unless it might be some feeble invalid in pursuit of pure air and of lost health. The sharp eyes of the latter-day seeker after hot-weather novelties, however, have peered into the varied delights of Nantucket; and now the story of its kindly and hospitable people, its varied sources of enjoyment, its health-restoring and invigorating sea-air, and the refreshing simplicity of its quaint, old-fashioned ways, so piquant because so new, — all this, and much more, is setting a strong tide of travel in the direction of that sandy home. Indeed, it may be feared that the bloom of its present freshness and novelty will soon be all worn away by the fast growing invasion; and Nantucket will be accounted one of the fashionable as well as health-giving resorts of the land. It is reached *viâ* the Old Colony Railroad and a line of steamers with which it connects.

Mattapoisett, a charming Massachusetts town, located on the shore of Buzzard's Bay, is deliciously rural, and not yet fashionable; but its surroundings promise much for the future. It may be reached by the Old Colony Road from Boston, and by the Fairhaven Branch from New Bedford.

Marion, a small but pretty place on Buzzard's Bay, has the partial regards of a limited number of travellers. Its facilities for boating, fishing, and shooting in the season make it a desirable resort for sportsmen.

Indeed, the seeker after quiet rural sports can scarcely go amiss, let him stop where he may along this pleasant coast. Its popularity is rapidly increasing; and each year adds to its accommodation for visitors.

New Bedford, of oleaginous fame the world over, is well worthy a sojourn from the summer tourist. Like Salem, New London, Newport, and Stonington, New Bedford was once the busy centre of a large and wealth-producing commerce, the whale-fishery being its chief industry. It still leads in this declining traffic; but its largely accumulated capital is rapidly seeking other and more profitable investments. It is noted for the prevailing air of good taste and refinement in its dwellings; and its future bids fair to maintain a long-established prestige. The city is reached by way of the "Old Colony" and the "Providence" and "Taunton Branch" Railroads.

The boats of the Martha's Vineyard line of steamers leave New Bedford daily, and furnish an additional variety to the sources of amusement in this popular region.

The Old Colony Railroad from Boston passes through Brockton, Taunton, Middleboro', and Fall River. At Fall River connection is made with the *Old Colony Steamboat Company's* splendid boats for New York; or the tourist may continue on the cars, and take the boat at Newport; or he can remain at Newport, for a visit to this unrivalled sea-shore resort.

Newport, R. I., is now the fashionable queen of all American watering resorts, for summer pleasure. With comparatively little of striking or romantic scenery, it has attractions peculiarly its own. Wealth and social distinction having approved of this really delightful location, the summer gatherings are of the gayest and most brilliant description. In elegance and splendor of outfit; in fame and beauty of its throngs; in all that invites the curious, the seekers after pleasure, the invalid's repose, and the glare and extravagance of fashion, — Newport is unrivalled. Indeed, this ancient and once renowned seat of commerce, after sinking into semi-oblivion, has been Rip-Van-Winkled into fame again, and is now in the bloom of a vigorous summer life, though still inclined to its winter drowse. The location of Fort Adams at Newport also adds to the attractiveness of the place.

NEWPORT, R.I.
Old Colony Steamboat Company's Docks.

From the south, Newport is reached by the Sound Steamers of the *Old Colony Steamboat Company,* "Fall River Line;" and from Boston by the "Old Colony" Road. Steamers also leave Providence for that city, stopping at all the leading places of interest along the shores of Narragansett Bay.

Perhaps in no particular has greater improvement been made in the last few years, than in the taste displayed in the construction of steamboats and railway cars, thus greatly lessening the fatigue and annoyance of travel. A journey may now be made without losing for a day the comforts of home. Cars and boats furnished with elegant parlors, inviting saloons, and luxuriant state-rooms, are now found on all the principal routes in America.

OLD COLONY STEAMBOAT COMPANY, "FALL RIVER LINE,"

Between New York and Boston, viâ Newport and Fall River.

The **Old Colony Steamboat Company** may well be said to occupy the front rank in this improvement; and its boats have no superiors in the world. Plying between the metropolis of the nation and the most fashionable watering-place on the continent, their saloons are constantly patronized by the *élite* of society.

Every afternoon long lines of carriages deposit their passengers at the company's wharf, PIER 28 (FOOT OF MURRAY STREET) NORTH RIVER, NEW YORK CITY; and at 5 P.M. in summer, and 4 P.M. in winter, the signal gun announces the hour of departure, and these magnificent floating palaces, crowded with human freight, glide into the stream. Martial music, by Hall's Boston Brass Band, enlivens the scene, as the gayly-dressed steamer majestically threads her way through the noble harbor, made rich in panoramic scenes by the marine of all nations. The twilight deepens as the stately vessel enters the East River, on her way to the placid waters of Long Island Sound. The scenery becomes beautified by the enchanting villas that line the shores, the homes of wealth and beauty; and nought is heard but the exclamations of delight from the assembled throng, the merry laugh of the promenaders, and the intoxicating strains of the reed and string music which have replaced the brass band. Thus into the night glides this living freight, — faith, comfort, and contentment resting in the minds of all.

The fleet of steamers formerly owned by the Narragansett Steamship Company (now by the "OLD COLONY") comprises the "Bristol," "Providence," "Old Colony," "Newport," "Metropolis," and "Empire State," — all of which are well known to the travelling public.

If we had not been warned by the march of improvement in the past, we should be tempted to believe that steamboat building has reached its climax in the superb vessels "Bristol" and "Providence."

On crossing the gang-plank the visitor finds himself on a broad deck, surrounded by richly carved and gilded panelling. The deck itself is composed of alternate strips of yellow pine and black walnut. In extreme width, this main deck measures eighty-four feet. Surrounding that portion of it which we enter from the wharf are the various offices for tickets, luggage, &c. Large doors in the after bulkhead lead to the ladies' saloons and state-rooms, which are appropriately divided for the use of ladies travelling alone, and for families with children, the most complete accommodations being provided for all. The main deck is divided into two general divisions by sliding glass doors. The forward part is used for freight; and the after part, which has just been described, is devoted to the use of passengers. From this after part, stairways lead to the upper and lower saloons. These stairs, with their highly-polished brass steps and their carved and graceful mahogany balusters, are separated from the open deck by a semicircular partition of woodwork and glass, which prevents the too strong draughts which a head wind sometimes occasions. Entering this semicircular enclosure, we descend to the lower saloon and supper-room. Here, in long perspective, tables, glittering with cut-glass and silver, stretch away toward the stern of the boat. Just forward of the stairway are the china-closet and kitchen, where all the culinary operations required on the boat are performed, and whose neat array of shining cooking utensils would delight the heart of the most fastidious housekeeper.

MAIN SALOON
Of the world-renowned Steamers "Bristol" and "Providence."

Leaving the appetizing scenes of the kitchen and supper-room, we ascend two broad and easy flights of stairs to the main saloon, which runs fore and aft nearly the whole length of the boat, with rows of staterooms on each side, and, in fact, overhead,—for there is yet another stairway, and another tier of state-rooms above us. The eight rooms which occupy the after part of the main saloon are for the accommodation of those who desire more luxurious surroundings than are sought by the public at large. These rooms far excel in elegance those of any first class hotel, and in size they are at least equal to the ordinary rooms of seaside houses. The other state-rooms, numbering in all three hundred, are large and well ventilated. They possess the peculiarity of having, in place of the ordinary fixed bunks, a kind of two-storied black walnut bedstead, which, being detached from the light woodwork, is comparatively free from the vibration commonly perceived when a steamboat is under way. Besides this provision against vibration, it will be observed that the partitions between the rooms are built diagonally; so that, instead of working with every revolution of the wheels, they form, in the aggregate, a powerful set of braces, adding much to the strength of the superstructure. The state-rooms of the upper tier are entered from broad galleries, which run around the saloon. These galleries unite at either end, and form spacious landings, on which are tables and chairs similar to those in the saloon; and the boats are lighted by the use of Bronner's patent gas-burners.

At 5.30, P.M., daily (Sundays, during the summer at 6.30), passengers for New York leave Boston, from the depot of the Old Colony Railroad, connecting with steamer at Fall River, leaving there at 7.15, P.M.; and at 8.15 in the evening the boat leaves Newport, arriving in New York in season to connect with all through trains South and West.

Passengers from New York, the West, or South, for any of the above places, can purchase tickets and have their baggage checked to destination; and by branch roads will be taken direct to any of the delightful resorts to which it leads, without the necessity of going to Boston.

Lake Champlain.— "This useful as well as beautiful sheet of water lies between the States of New York and Vermont, and extends a short distance into Canada. It is, in extreme length, about one hundred and thirty miles, and varies in width from half a mile to fifteen miles, the water, in places, being near three hundred feet deep. The Vermont shores of the lake are generally fertile and well cultivated; while those of New York are wild, rocky, and barren, rising into vast mountains, and contain rich iron deposits.

"The shores of Lake Champlain are not only interesting in themselves, but they hold many places of celebrity and attractiveness. The ruins of old Fort Ticonderoga stand out upon a high, rocky cliff at the confluence of the outlet of Lake George with Lake Champlain. The remains of the fortress at Crown Point loom up opposite to Chimney Point. The localities where Burgoyne held his famous Indian council and made his treaty, and where Arnold fought with Carleton, are pointed out. **Plattsburg,** the scene of the battles on the 11th of September, 1814, in which Commodore McDonough gained his signal naval victory, and General Macomb compelled Sir George Prevost to retire into Canada, is the most conspicuous and interesting point on the lake. Numerous natural curiosities exist on its islands and shores; but space will not permit their mention here. Burlington, a beautiful city on the Vermont shore, is well worth the attention of tourists. From Plattsburg the Adirondacks are reached with facility; and it is a starting-point for Au Sable Chasm, one of the most remarkable curiosities in the United States."

ETTYSBURG

PUBLICATIONS,

BY

JOHN B. BACHELDER,

57 Beekman Street, New York.
41-45 Franklin Street, Boston.

A MAGNIFICENT OIL PAINTING

AND
STEEL ENGRAVING

OF THE

REPULSE OF LONGSTREET'S ASSAULT,

THE DECISIVE MOMENT OF THE

BATTLE OF GETTYSBURG.

Painted by JAMES WALKER,

From Historical Designs by John B. Bachelder.

This painting is 20 feet long and 7½ feet high, and is unquestionably

THE FINEST BATTLE SCENE IN AMERICA.

It has been on exhibition thirty-one months, has been examined by thousands of soldiers without the discovery of a mistake, and has received the unqualified approval of military men and art critics.

A MAGNIFICENT STEEL ENGRAVING,

FROM IT, IN LINE,

By H. B. HALL, Jr.

A work of superior merit, 35 inches long, engraved surface, and executed in the

HIGHEST STYLE OF ART.

PRICES.

ELECTROTYPE EDITION	$ 7.50
PRINT	15.00
PLAIN PROOF, on superior plate paper	25.00
INDIA PROOF, on fine India paper	50.00
ARTIST PROOF (limited to two hundred copies)	100.00

Sold only by Subscription.

TWENTY-ONE THOUSAND SEVEN HUNDRED AND FIFTY DOLLARS WORTH already ordered!!

PUBLISHED BY

JOHN B. BACHELDER,

41–45 Franklin St., Boston; 57 Beekman St., New York.

 # ILLUSTRATED HISTORY

OF THE
BATTLE OF GETTYSBURG.

BY
JOHN B. BACHELDER.

It is unquestionably true that a very much better idea of a battle will be derived if the text is illustrated by portraits of the actors, and engravings of the action. Such a representation of the Battle of Gettysburg is nearly ready for press, and when finished will make a most

COMPLETE HISTORY OF THE BATTLE

It forms a beautiful portrait album of the generals in command. OVER NINETY-ONE HUNDRED DOLLARS' WORTH ARE ALREADY ENGRAVED, including magnificent Steel Portraits of Generals

MEADE,	STANNARD,	HAYS,	WHEATON,	GEARY,	McGILVERY,
REYNOLDS,	HANCOCK,	SHERRILL,	BARTLETT,	GREENE,	PLEASANTON,
NEWTON,	ZOOK,	BULL,	HOWARD,	KANE,	BUTTERFIELD,
WADSWORTH,	GIBBON,	VINCENT,	AMES,	HUNT,	WARREN,
MEREDITH,	WEBB,	CRAWFORD,	SLOCUM,	RANDOLPH,	INGALLS.
DOUBLEDAY	HALL,	WRIGHT,	WILLIAMS,	MARTIN,	

And others ordered.

Portraits of General Lee and his Corps and Division Commanders
Will be introduced. Also Wood-Cut Illustrations of

SOME OF THE MOST THRILLING EPISODES OF THE BATTLE

These engravings have been furnished by friends of the parties interested, as manifestations of their esteem.

PRICES FOR INTRODUCING ILLUSTRATIONS. — *Steel Portraits*, $150. *Wood-Cuts*, $5, $25, or $75, according to size, invariably in advance. Parties wishing portraits or wood-cuts should write immediately.

PRICES OF HISTORY.

```
POPULAR EDITION, without portraits, bound in cloth............................$5.00
     "         "    with portraits printed from transfers...................... 7.50
LIBRARY        "    royal octavo, good paper, bound in sheep.................. 12.00
HALF MOROCCO EDITION, fine paper, proof portraits, beveled boards............ 17.50
FINE EDITION, tinted paper, proof portraits, full morocco, beveled boards, gilt... 25.00
LARGE PAPER EDITION, printed from large, new type, original wood-cuts, hand-
   press, heavy toned calendered paper, INDIA PROOF portraits, in sheets, uncut..100.00
Elaboratey bound, full levant morocco, gilt................................... 125.00
```

JOHN B. BACHELDER,
41-45 Franklin St., Boston; 57 Beekman St., New York.
189

INDEX.

Absecon, N.J., 58.
Adirondack Mountains, N.Y., 144.
Alexandria Bay, N.Y., 54.
Allentown, Penn., 35, 36.
Alton Bay, N.H., 19.
Altoona, Penn., 135.
Ammonoosuc Falls, 121.
Ammonoosuc River, 109.
Andover, Mass, 17.
Ashland, N.H., 104.
Ashley, Penn., 51.
Atlantic House, Me., 28.
Augusta Springs, Va., 164.
Baker's River, N.H., 105.
Bald Head Cliff, 28.
Ballardvale, Mass., 17.
Baltimore and Potomac Railway, 72.
Baltimore, Md., 72.
Bartlett, N.H., 26.
Basin, N.H., 106.
Bath Alum Springs, Va., 164.
Bath, N.H., 109
Bay View House, Alton Bay, N.H , 19.
Bay View House, Laconia, N.H., 95, 98.
Bear Mountain, Penn., 41.
Beaver Meadow, Penn., 48.
Bedford Springs, Penn., 64.
Beecher's Falls, White Mountains, 119.
Belknap Mountain, N.H., 22, 98.
Bellows Falls, Vt., 64.
Belmont, N.H., 95.
Belvidere Railroad, 35.
Berkley Springs, Va , 164.
Berwick, Me., 28.
Bethlehem, N.H., 112.
Bethlehem, Penn., 36.
Biddeford, Me., 29.
Binghamton, N.Y., 35.
Boar's Head, N.H., 90.
Boston and Maine Railroad, 17, 26, 91.
Boston, City of, 143.
Boston, Concord, & Montreal R.R., 26, 91-122.
Bradford, Mass., 17.
Bridgeport, Penn., 75.
Buzzard s Bay, Mass., 167.
Camden and Atlantic Railroad, 58.
Campton, N.H., 106.
Canterbury, N.H., 95.
Canton, Penn., 77.
Cape Arundel, Me., 29.
Cape Cod, Mass., 180.
Cape Elizabeth, Me., 31.
Cape May, N.J., 55.
Cape Porpoise, Me., 28.
Capon Springs, West Va., 164.
Casco Bay, Me., 69.
Catawissa Railroad, 47.
Catskill Mountains, N.Y., 140.
Central Railroad of New Jersey, 34-53.
Centre Harbor, N.H., 24, 100.
Chelsea, Mass., 90.
Chelsea (Revere) Beach, 90.
Chemung River, N.Y., 78.
Chicago, Burlington, and Quincy R.R., 66.
Chocorua Mountain, N.H., 22.

Clifton Springs, N.Y., 154.
Cloud Point, Penn., 50.
Coal Mining, 46.
Coatesville Bridge, Penn., 125.
Cocheco River, N.H., 19.
Cohasset, Mass., 178.
Columbia Branch Railroad, 73, 133.
Columbia Springs, N.Y., 140.
Concord, N.H., 17, 93.
Concord Railroad, N.H., 19, 91.
Connecticut River, 109.
Connecticut River and Passumpsic Railroad, 91.
Conway, N.H., 100.
Cooperstown, N.Y., 32.
Copple-Crown Mountain, N.H., 22.
Cotuit Port, Mass., 180.
Crawford House, White Mountains, 119.
Cresson, Penn., 136.
Crystal Cascade, N.H., 124.
Cumberland Valley Railroad, 137.
Cushing's Island, Me., 65.
Dalton, N.H., 111.
Danvers, Mass., 17.
Deer Isle, Me., 69.
Delaware, Lack'a, and West. R.R., 35, 158.
Delaware and Hudson Railroad, 53.
Delaware Water Gap, 35, 131, 132.
Doubling Gap White Sulphur Springs, 54.
Dover, N.H., 19, 28.
Dover and Winnepesaukee Railroad, 19.
Durham, N.H., 19.
Dutchman's Run, Penn., 77.
Duxbury, Mass., 178.
Eagle Hotel, Concord, N.H., 93.
Eastern Railroad, 21, 32.
Easton, Penn., 35.
Ebensburg, Penn., 90.
Echo Lake, N H., 106.
Edgartown, Mass., 172.
Egg Harbor City, N.J., 58.
Elizabeth Islands, 167.
Elmira, N.Y., 78.
Empire Fall, N.Y., 80.
Erie, Penn , 76.
Erie Railroad, 78.
Exeter, N.H., 19.
Fabyan House, White Mountains, 116-119.
Fairhaven, Mass., 167.
Fairmount Park, Philadelphia, 128.
Falmouth Heights, Mass., 167, 180.
Flume, Franconia, N.H., 106.
Framingham and Lowell Railroad, 91.
Franconia Notch, N.H., 105.
Frost's Point, N.H., 65.
Ganoga Falls, North Mountain, Penn., 158.
Gay Head, Mass., 167.
Genesee Falls, N.Y., 65.
Georgetown, Mass., 17.
Gettysburg, Penn., 73.
Gibbs Falls, White Mountains, 119.
Gilmanton, N.H., 19, 95.
Glendon House, Wolfboro, 21.
Glen Ellis Falls, N.H., 124.
Glen Excelsior, N.Y., 80.

INDEX. 191

Glen Mountain House, Watkins Glen, 81.
Glen's Falls, N.Y., 123.
Glen Thomas, 51.
Glen, White Mountains, N.H., 124.
Gloucester, Mass., 11, 165.
Great Bend, 35.
Great Falls, N.H., 28.
Greenbrier White Sulphur Sp'gs, Va., 164.
Green Ridge, Penn., 53.
Greenwood Lake, N.Y., 33.
Greenwood, Mass., 17.
Gunstock Mountain, N.H., 22.
Halifax, N.C., 11.
Hampton Junction, N.J., 35.
Hampton, N.H., 19, 90.
Hanover Junction, Penn., 73.
Herdic House, Williamsport, Penn., 76.
Harrisburg, Penn., 35, 36, 75, 134.
Hathaway House, Elmira, N.Y., 79.
Havana, N.Y., 80.
Haverhill, Mass., 17.
" N.H., 109.
Hazelton, Penn., 48.
Healing Springs, Va., 164.
Hector Falls, N.Y., 87.
Hingham, Mass., 179.
Hooksett, N.H., 92.
Hot Springs, Va., 164.
Howe's Cave, N.Y., 70.
Hudson River, N.Y., 138.
Hyannis, Mass, 179.
Island Ledge House, Me., 28.
Isles of Shoals, N.H., 89.
Illinois Central Railroad, 67.
Jefferson, N.H., 112.
Jones's Falls, Baltimore, Md., 73.
Jordan Rock Alum Springs, Va., 164.
Katama, Mass., 172.
Kennebeck River, 11.
Kennebunk, Me., 28.
Kennebunkport, Me., 29.
Kiarsarge House, North Conway, N.H., 13.
Kiarsarge Mountain, 13.
Kingston, R.I., 89.
Lackawanna and Bloomsburg Railroad, 53.
Laconia, N.H., 95.
"Lady of the Lake" (Steamer), 26, 98, 101.
Lake Champlain, 186.
Lake George, N.Y., 124, 140.
Lake Roland, Md., 73.
Lake Village, N.H., 98.
Lake Winnepesaukee, N.H., 19.
Lancaster, N.H., 111.
Lancaster House, N.H., 111.
Lancaster, Penn., 73.
Lawrence, Mass., 17.
Lehigh and Lackawanna Railroad, 36.
Lehigh and Susquehanna Railroad, 35.
Lehigh Valley, 34-53.
Lehigh Valley Railroad, 78.
Libbey's Neck, 64.
Lisbon, N.H., 109.
Little Boar's Head, N.H., 70.
Littleton, N.H., 108.
Livermore Falls, N.H., 105.
Logan House, Altoona, Penn., 136.
Long Branch, N.J., 33.
Long Island, Mass., 11.
Long Island, N.Y., 140.
Loretto, Penn., 137.
Lowell Island, Mass., 89.
Lycoming Creek, Penn., 76.
Lynn, Mass., 68.
Malden, Mass., 17.
Manch Chunk, Penn., 35-47.

Manchester and Lawrence Railroad, 91.
Manchester, N.H., 17, 91.
Manhanset House, Shelter Isl'd, N.Y., 146.
Mansion House, Manch Chunk, Penn., 39.
Maplewood House, Bethlehem, N.H., 113.
Marblehead, Mass., 89.
Marion, Mass., 182.
Marshfield, Mass., 178.
Martha's Vineyard, 166-176.
"Martha's Vineyard" (Steamboat), 166.
Mattakeset Lodge, Mass., 172.
Mattapoisett, Mass., 182.
Merrimac River, N.H., 93.
Minnequa Springs, Penn., 77.
Mohawk River, 32.
Montgomery White Sulphur Sp'gs, Va., 164.
Montmorenci Falls, 165.
Moosehead Lake, Me., 165.
Moosilauke Mountain, N.H., 106.
Morris and Essex Railroad, 35.
Moultonboro, N.H., 26.
Mount Carmel, Penn., 75.
Mount Clinton, N.H., 120.
Mount Desert, Me., 11, 68.
Mount Holly Springs, Penn., 54.
Mount Lafayette, N.H., 106.
Mount Monroe, N.H., 120.
Mount Pisgah, Penn., 42.
Mount Pleasant, N.H., 120.
Mount Prospect, N.H., 105, 117.
Mount Vernon, Va., 11.
Mount Washington, N.H., 19, 120.
"Mount Washington" (Steamer), 19, 26.
Mount Washington Railway, 121.
Mount Washington Summit House, 116, 122.
Mount Webster, N.H., 120.
Mount Willard, N.H., 119.
Mountain House, Cresson, Pa., 136.
Moyer's Rock, Manch Chunk, Pa., 45.
Nahant, Mass., 11, 123.
Nantasket Beach, Mass., 11, 178.
Nauticote Railroad, 53.
Nantucket, Mass., 184.
Narraganset Pier, R.I., 89.
Nescopec Railroad, 48.
Nesquehoning Valley Railroad, 47.
New Bedford, Mass., 167, 182.
New Lebanon Springs, N.Y., 140.
New London, Conn., 89.
New Market, N.H., 19.
New Market Junction, N.H., 19.
New York City, 138.
Newbury, Vt., 109.
Newburyport, Mass., 17, 70.
Newport, R.I., 183.
Niagara Falls, 88, 153.
North Conway, N.H., 12, 21, 26.
North Hampton, N.H., 70.
North Mountain, Penn., 35.
North Mountain House, Penn., 53, 155-163.
North Pennsylvania Railroad, 36.
Northern Central Railroad, 71-88, 134.
Northumberland, N.H., 112.
Oak Bluffs and Katama, Mass., 166-176, 184.
Old Colony Railroad, 167, 177-186.
Old Colony Steamboat Company, 184-186.
Old Orchard Beach, Me., 29, 64.
Omaha, 69.
Onoko Station, Manch Chunk, Penn., 43, 44.
Ossipee Falls, N.H., 22.
Ossipee Mountain, N.H., 22.
Otsego Lake, N.Y., 32, 123.
Owl's Head, N.H., 109.
Pavilion Hotel, Wolfboro, N.H., 21, 22.
Pemigewasset House, Plymouth, N.H., 104.

Pemigewasset River, N.H., 102.
Penn Haven, Penn., 48.
Pennsylvania Railroad. 36, 125-137.
Penobscot River, 11.
Philadelphia, Penn., 75.
Philadelphia and Erie Railroad, 75, 76, 134.
Philipsburg, N.J., 35.
Pigeon Cove, Mass., 165.
Pittsburg, Penn., 35, 137.
Pittsfield, N.H., 19.
Plaistow, N.H., 17.
Plum Island, Mass., 70.
Plymouth, Mass., 178.
Plymouth, N.H., 26, 103-106.
Pool, Franconia, N.H., 106.
Portage, N.Y., 144.
Portland and Ogdensburg Railroad, 13, 116.
Portland, Me., 19, 31, 64.
Portsmouth and Concord Railroad, 19, 91.
Portsmouth, N.H., 65.
Profile House, N.H., 106, 111.
Profile, Franconia, N.H., 106.
Prospect Rock, Penn., 49.
Prout's Neck, Me., 64.
Providence Railroad, 142.
Provincetown, Mass., 179.
Quantico, Va., 72.
Ragged Mountain. N.H., 102.
Rainbow Falls, Watkins Glen, N.Y., 86.
Ralston, Penn., 76.
Rawley Springs, Va., 164.
Reading, Mass., 17.
Reading, Penn., 35.
Red Hill, N.H., 24, 98.
Renova Springs, Penn., 76.
"Rhode Island" (Steamer), 142.
Richfield Springs, N.Y., 123.
Richmond, Fredericksburg, and Potomac Railroad, 72.
Roaring Creek, Penn., 77.
Rockbridge Alum Springs, Va., 164.
Rockbridge Baths, Va., 164.
Rockport, Mass., 165.
Rocky Point, R.I., 32
Rollingsford, N.H., 28.
Rye Beach, N H., 32, 144.
Saco, Me., 29, 78.
Saco Pool, 29.
Saguenay River, 165.
Sanbornton Bridge, N.H., 95.
Sandford's Independent Line Steamers, 11.
Sandwich Mountains, N.H., 22.
Sandwich, N.H., 26.
Salem and Lowell Railroad, 17.
Salem, Mass., 54.
Salmon Falls, N.H., 28.
Saratoga Springs. N.Y., 151.
Scarborough Beach, Me., 31, 144.
Scranton, Penn., 35, 53.
Schuyler's Lake, N.Y., 123.
Sea View House, Mass., 169.
Seneca Falls, N.Y., 69.
Seneca Lake, N.Y., 88.
Senter House, N.H., 24.
Shamokin, Penn., 75.
Sharon Springs, N.Y., 65, 70.
Shelter Island, N.Y., 145-150.
Silver Cascade, White Mountains, N H., 119.
Solomon's Gap, Penn., 51, 52.
Somerville, Mass., 17.
South Newmarket, N.H., 19.
Squam Lake, N.H., 25, 102.
Squam River, N.H., 102.
Star Island, Isles of Shoals, 154.
"Star of the East" (steamer), 11.

Steamer "Mount Washington," 19.
Stockton House, Cape May, N.J., 55.
Stoneham, Mass., 17.
Stonington, Conn., 70.
Stonington Steamboat Line, 70, 141.
Straw's Point, N.H., 32.
Summit Hill, Penn., 44.
Summit House, Moosilauke Mt, N.H., 107
Sunbury, Penn., 75.
Suncook Valley Railroad, 19, 93.
Suspension Bridge, N.Y., 69.
Susquehanna River, 74.
Swampscott, Mass., 68.
Sweet Springs, Va., 164.
Switch-back Railroad, 41.
Taghkanic Falls, N.Y., 65.
Tamworth, N.H., 26.
Taunton Branch Railroad, 182.
Tekaharawa Falls, N.Y., 70.
Thousand Islands, 54.
Tilton, N.H., 94.
Tinker's Island, Mass., 89.
Trenton Falls, N.Y., 32.
Troy, Penn., 78.
Tuckerman's Ravine, N.H., 120.
Tumble-down-Dick Mountain, N.H., 22.
Twin Mountain House, N.H., 114.
Union Bridge, N.H., 95.
Union Pacific Railroad, 68.
Vineyard Haven, Mass., 168
Virginia Springs, 164.
Wakefield, Mass., 17.
Warren, N.H., 107.
Warm Springs, Va., 164.
Washington, D.C., 11, 71.
Washington's Rock, N.J., 35.
Watch Hill Point, R.I., 124.
Watkins Glen, N.Y., 35, 81-88.
Waukawan Lake, N.H., 102.
Waumbec House, N.H., 112.
Weir's Landing, N.H., 99.
Wells Beach, Me., 28, 70.
Wells River, Vt., 109.
West Amesbury, Mass., 19.
West Canada Creek, N.Y., 32.
West Jersey Railroad, 55.
West Ossipee, N.H., 26.
Western Travel, 66.
White Mountains, N.H., 19.
White Mountain Notch, 119.
Whitefield, N.H., 111.
Wilkes Barre, Penn., 35.
Willey Notch, White Mountains, 119.
Williamsport, Penn., 35, 47, 76.
Wilmington and Baltimore Railroad, 72.
Wilmington Junction, Mass., 17.
Wing Branch Railroad, 111.
Winnesquam House, N.H., 95.
Winnesquam Lake, 95.
Winnipesaukee Lake, N.H., 19, 95.
Winnipesaukee River, 95.
Wissahickon River, Philadelphia, 128.
Wolfboro, N.H., 24, 100.
Wolfboro Branch Railroad, 21.
Woods Hole, Mass., 167, 181.
Woodstock, N.H., 106.
Woodsville, N.H., 109.
Worcester and Nashua Railroad, 91.
Wrightsville Branch Railroad, 73.
Wyoming Valley Hotel, Penn., 53.
Yellow Sulphur Springs, Va., 164.
York Beach, Me., 124.
York, Penn., 73.
York, Penn. Branch Railroad, 133.
York Springs, Penn., 54.

www.ingramcontent.com/pod-product-compliance
Lightning Source LLC
Chambersburg PA
CBHW020847160426
43192CB00007B/812